Special Dedication to my Mother and Father

Love Lucille

DEDICATION

I dedicate this book to those I have enjoyed cooking for. I pray that you feel my love and passion for the art of hospitality and making people happy through food. I also want to encourage anyone at any age with a dream or plan lying dormant somewhere in a drawer collecting dust, for it is in these seemingly forgotten dreams that the most beautiful accomplishments can be born. Shake off the dust and pursue the dream until it becomes an accomplishment. I dedicate this book to my seven children, without whom life would have no meaning.

I would like first to thank my Lord and Savior, Jesus Christ, for allowing me to see 96 years. Never in my wildest dreams did I ever expect to live this long? I've lost so many friends and family members. Recently, I've lost two sisters. But this book is not about what I have lost but what I have gained. Through the generosity of my daughter Tonia, I have been blessed to take several cruises to Mexico and the Caribbean.

I visited the beautiful Hilton Head Island with Diane, Ed, and my grandchildren, my son Michael and Tonya. Bonita has always seen that I have everything that I need. There are so many places that I never dreamed that I would ever be able to visit. Everyone who knows me knows how proud I am of my children—Barbara, my youngest daughter who served her country in the Navy. Diane's affiliation with The Republic of Benin introduced me to African kings and presidents and her singing career on several continents—Bonita's apartment housing development designed to house those in the disabled community. Tonia's yearly trips to Las Vegas, Michael for his ability to do excellent home remodeling, and Tiffany and Karla for their love and devotion to me. I love them and am proud of them all.

One thing about life Is that you never know what awaits; you can only pray and ask God to help you go down the right path. There is no book or guide on raising children, but I always knew God would care for them.

Even when unsure of the next step, I've taught them to reach the one who can guide them on the right path. I am the oldest of five children by my mother and father, yet I am the only one still living. I miss my sisters and brother dearly. I miss my friends and family members.

I miss my husband; he passed away before he could share our golden years. He left before he could marvel at the accomplishments of his children and grandchildren. As he watched the 1984 Bowl between the Washington Redskins and the Los Angeles Raiders. Joe died in bed. The Raiders won 38 – 9.

God has kept me here for a purpose, and I do not want to miss out. I want to be found worthy of the assignment. Life is like the four Seasons. In the summer of our youth, we spend our early years trying to find purpose. We enter our spring season with determination and an agenda for life, and our choices become wiser and more metered, heading toward our chosen pathways. It's usually at this time of our lives that we seek something greater than ourselves. Most of us find it in Jesus Christ, but not all. In our fall, we are older, carrying the regrets and scars gained along the way. There are disappointments, losses, and rebounds, and in our winter season, there is a settling. Because we know that there are more years behind us than ahead. We want our lives to matter; we need to leave a legacy.

We want to be remembered as someone who tried to make life better for all we encountered. In our humanity, we may have more losses than wins. Where is our deliverer who can give us a life of peace, right our wrongs, and reconcile us back to God? The Apostle Paul said in Romans 7:24, "Who will rescue me from this body that is subject to death?" He said: "Thanks be to God, who delivers me through Jesus Christ our Lord!" The deliverance from sin and death comes through faith in Jesus Christ and the indwelling presence of the Holy Spirit.

Jesus looks past our mistakes or sins and covers them with his blood, so we become God's righteousness in Christ Jesus. I have been writing down little passages of my life and sharing them openly with you—unashamed because God has taken me on a journey where I can look back and say that, too, has passed. I want to leave a legacy for my children, family, loved ones, and those who know me. Lucille could cook, was enthusiastic and compassionate, and loved her children and family. I may not remember everything about my past, but I am sure of my future. "For the Lord himself shall descend from heaven with a shout, with the voice of the archangel, and with the trump of God: and the dead in Christ shall rise first:" 1 Thessalonians 4:6.

Thank You

I want to thank all of you who have shown interest in this book. I pray that you find something of value in it. Hopefully, there are some nuggets of wisdom, lessons learned, inspiration, and a desire for a closer walk with God. When the Good Lord asks me at the Pearly Gates, Lucille, what did you do with the long life I blessed you with? I will answer that I did all I could for my children, served in church, cherished my family and friends, and loved you, Jesus, with all my heart. I dedicate this book to my seven children, grandchildren, and great-grandchildren, without whom life would be meaningless.

The Beginning

I was born October 5th, 1927. My parents rented a house from Ms. Ethel Lee Lindsey of Oak and Page in Malvern, Arkansas. The month before my birth, the mighty Mississippi River unleashed destructive flooding across the United States from Illinois to Arkansas on an Easter Sunday. I was told the angry waters poured into Arkansas when the levees broke near Poplar Bluff, Missouri, and continued its wreckage until it subsided in September.

The Malvern Daily Record records sunny and 88 degrees the day Dr. Barrier, a renowned physician from Pulaski County, delivered the first child of 30-year-old Hartsell and 22-year-old Louise Smith. My birth was the calm after the storm. I have two younger sisters, Lillian and Latora, and one brother, Titus. I was the oldest of the bunch; however, I am still determining if I could be called a role model. I was always adventurous and walked to the beat of my drum, but I loved my family. We shared a four-room home on Banks Street. The house was built in the late 1800s for a city teacher in Malvern. Growing up, our lives were good.

My parents were loving people who raised their children to believe in God and look out for one another. Momma grew a garden, and we had plenty of fresh vegetables on our dinner table: purple hull peas, okra, squash, tomatoes, and more. We raised chickens and always had fresh eggs. My youthful foundation was spending summers playing outside with my friends and cousins, picking figs, fishing in the nearby creeks, and going to Bethel A.M.E. Church on Sundays. I often helped my mother, watching her cook. They said my mom was the prettiest Black woman in Malvern. Her long hair, which she occasionally wore down or up in a twist, framed her beautiful face. She would cook and sing in the purest soprano voice. The Southern gospel was always on the radio as she cleaned and moved around the kitchen, but the choirs and vocalists on the radio were no match for the angelic sounds coming from my mother.

Lucille Cameron

x

My mother and father, Hartsell & Louise Smith (Gloster)

Heritage

I come from an esteemed genealogy: the Smiths from Tulip, Arkansas, Glosters (who originated from Ireland), Greens, Morgans, Beards, Camerons, Hudson's, Jones, McNeely's, and claimed kinship of the families related to them. Writing This & That is a lesson of self-discovery.

My tender yearnings for God and emotional love letters were written with the innocence of a young bride separated from her true love by war or distance.

In these pages, I hope has wisdom and wise counsel like the griots my daughter would tell me about in Africa. The elders would sit at a respected place near the village gates and provide wise counsel to those looking for answers to the thorns in their lives. The comparison may be exaggerated; let us call it poetic license. I had some early life hardships, but God mends brokenness. Hopefully, my candidness will comfort those going through what I did. My children didn't want me to tell one story, but this book would not have been authentic without it. We should never be ashamed of our youthful folly; we make better choices and decisions as we mature. I am not ashamed of growth; change is a part of life.

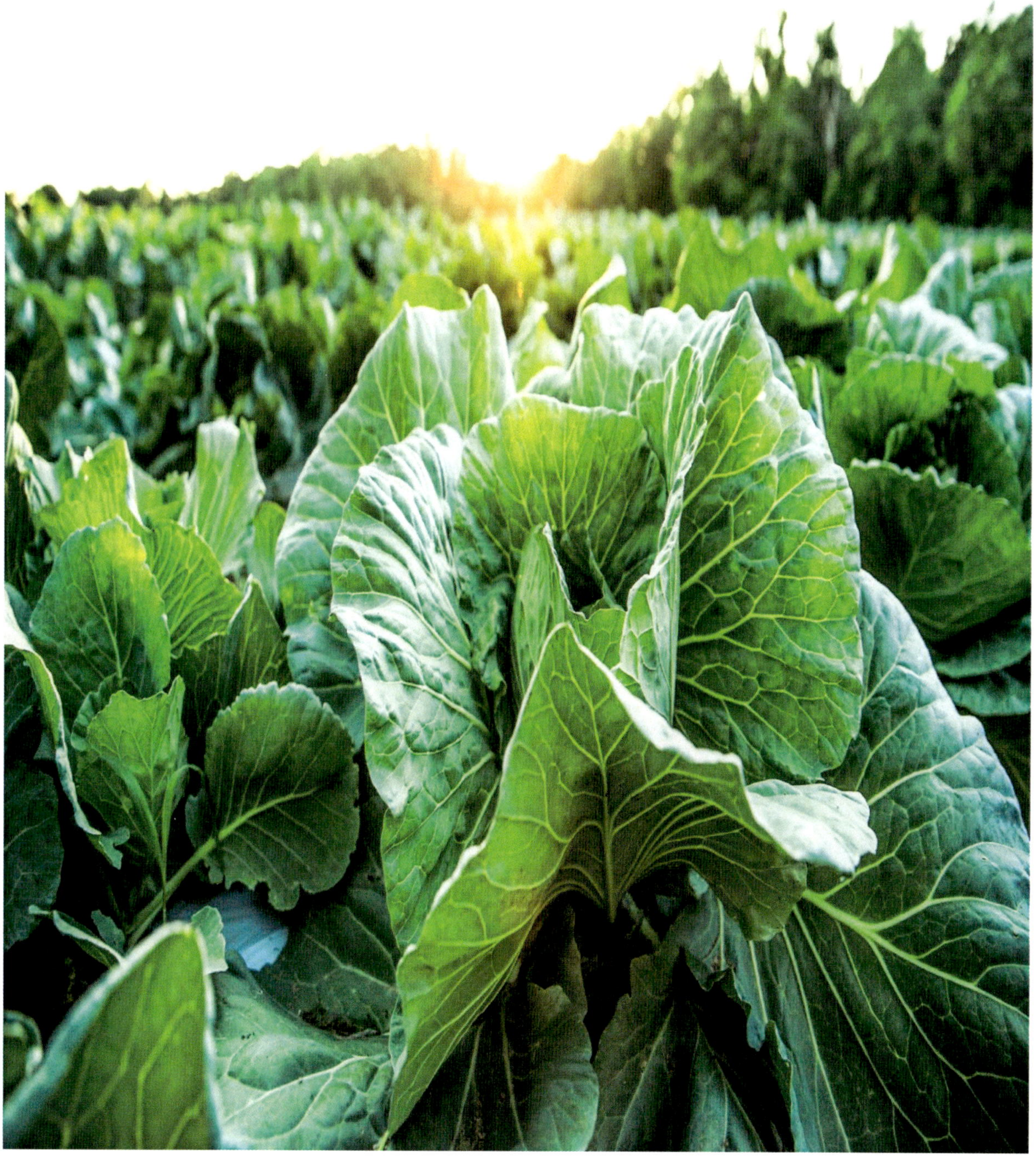

My grandmother Elsie Gloster (nee: Green)

My Daddy

When I was born, I was told my daddy brought people off the street to look at his baby. I was his first; a lady told me you were a little ugly squinch-eyed baby. In 1930, President Franklin D. Roosevelt came to Malvern; Daddy carried me on his shoulder to see the parade down Fourth Street. I was three years old. I remember sitting on my mother's lap as she read to me from a storybook made of cloth. I remember getting whipped by my mother because I had a smart mouth. One day, we went to JCPenney's in town. I wanted something; I cannot remember what it was. My sister Latora witnessed the event, and over the years, we would share a laugh when it came up. Well, my mom would not buy it. I got on the floor and had a tantrum. I did that often, and it worked. I wanted to go to Rockport one day, and I started shaking like I was having a seizure. It was not long before I was on my way to Rockport. I wanted to go to another place but don't recall where; my father told me I could go, but only if my sister Latora went. Daddy gave me a curfew, but naturally, I stayed late, and my father came to look for us. I saw him coming across the street, and I started to walk like a disabled person, and he did not recognize me. If I had been in Hollywood, I would have won the Academy Award before Hattie McDaniel.

Celeste and Juanita

My cousins, Juanita and Celeste, took me to school with them even though I was too young to go. I remember their teacher instructing them in Latin perfectly. I was clever, so I learned along with them. My mother dressed me cute; I had long, braided hair and wore ribbons.

My cousins taught me how to style it, and as I got older. I started spending summers in Little Rock with my mother's cousins Viola and James Thornton. My mother's sisters needed a babysitter for Heloise and Lindsay Branch. My aunt took me to Little Rock, and I refused to return to Malvern. I met Eloise Swinton; we became close friends. We would go to the YMCA, play ping pong, and spend time together. Her mother's name was Mary Lewis, and her excellent cooking reminded me of my mother's.

Pauline

Pauline came to live with us; we were like sisters. I love Malvern. But I loved Little Rock even more. To me, it was high society. I would bloom from a young girl to a young woman there. Pauline and I were very civic minded to be so young we would read the Little Rock Black news publication, the Arkansas World. All my life, I have been an armchair activist. I was pleased to see my daughters adopt a natural hairstyle as they grew into teenagers. Pauline and I adapted to the segregationist lifestyle prevalent everywhere in Arkansas; even in our beloved Little Rock, we did not like it, but we endured it.

We conformed, but I knew there was a better life somewhere else. We would sit in the living room and sing "Don't Fence Me In" by Gene Autry.

Recalling the lyrics now, the line "I can't stand fences" was a plea to live without boundaries or limitations. It could have been a desire to live beyond the constraints impeded by discrimination or be free. Once summer was over, I went back to school in Malvern. It was years later before I saw Pauline again. Life separated us, but we will meet again.

7th Grade

My teacher in 7th grade was Helen Williams. I've always been a quick learner. So, out of all the students in the class, she made me conjugate verbs on the blackboard. She also had me stand before the class to recite verses from various poetry books. I thought she was mean and did not like me because she made me learn. Later in life, I reflected on her insistence that I know how to speak correctly. I am sending a big tribute to Helen Williams and the teachers who care. A big salute to all the educators who were influential in the lives of their students because they cared. She probably never knew that one of her students would, at 92, still remember her name. Thank you, Ms. Helen!

My Story

I am the first child of Hartsell and Louise Smith, born and raised in Malvern, Arkansas, into a loving and God-fearing family. I am the big sister to the late Lillian Beard (Herbert), the late Titus Henry Smith (Billie), the late Latora Morgan (Reuben), and our oldest brother, Samuel (God rest his soul). As the mother of five children, I marveled at them entering their chosen career fields. When you become a mother, your most important mission is helping your children find their life's journey. I stored my dreams in a shoe box to raise my five children, including my two bonus daughters, whom I love as my own. It was to be a recipe book with memoirs of all the weddings, private dinners, graduations, luaus, clubs, church, and civic events I catered. But I decided I had a story to tell—a story of life experiences, relationships, and lessons I learned. So, I named it a little bit of this and a little bit of that, and I am finally settling on This & That. This is not a novel or a fictional tale. Instead, it is a snapshot of my life in memoirs in pictures, prose, poetry, and recipes. It is a timeline of the 90-plus years that the Good Lord has allowed me to breathe his air. I am deeply grateful for all my family, children, grandchildren, great-grand, nieces, nephews, their families, cousins, and dearly departed loved ones, to whom I was also blessed to be part of their lives.

Daily.

I have loving memories of my mother and Father, Aunts & Uncles, Big Momma and Daddy Raymond, Fran, Etta, Helen, Carolyn, Eloise, Ms. Redding, Omar, Ms. Crawford, Ms. Neely, Ms. Baskett, Ms. Chaney, Ms. King, Cousin Ola Fay in California, Sandra, Jackie, Irene, Clara. Ma-Dear, Jo-Ethel, Patty & Dr. Ashford, Dr. Love Cheryl Batts, Bertha, Pastor Chester Jones, Juana, Ms. Springer, Ms. Crigler, Mr. Beard, Ms. Al-Amin, Rose, Zack, Dick, Humphrey, Hazel, Roy, Lil, their children, and their families. My husband, Joe, his brothers, and their wives and families. Big Ma, Uncle Bruce, Sweetening, Dolly, Doris, Alma, Pearl, Janice, Pearline on. I am thankful for my Hot Springs, Little Rock friends, and many others who remain unnamed. When I hear that final trump of God, it is time for me to receive my eternal rest. Don't grieve, but celebrate my life, for it has been well lived. If I inadvertently omitted anyone's name, you are still loved. I apologize. Just wait until you get 96 and see how good your memory is.

Lucille Cameron

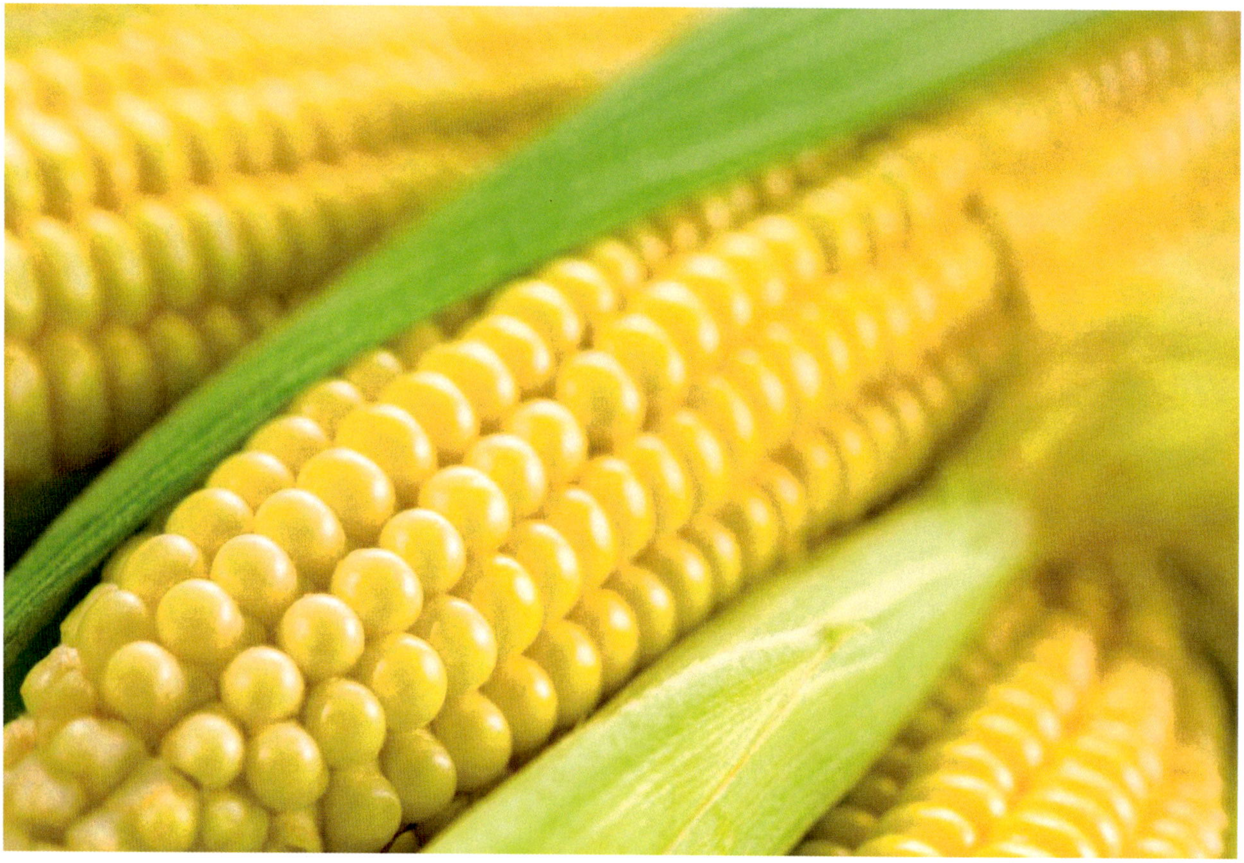

Growing Up

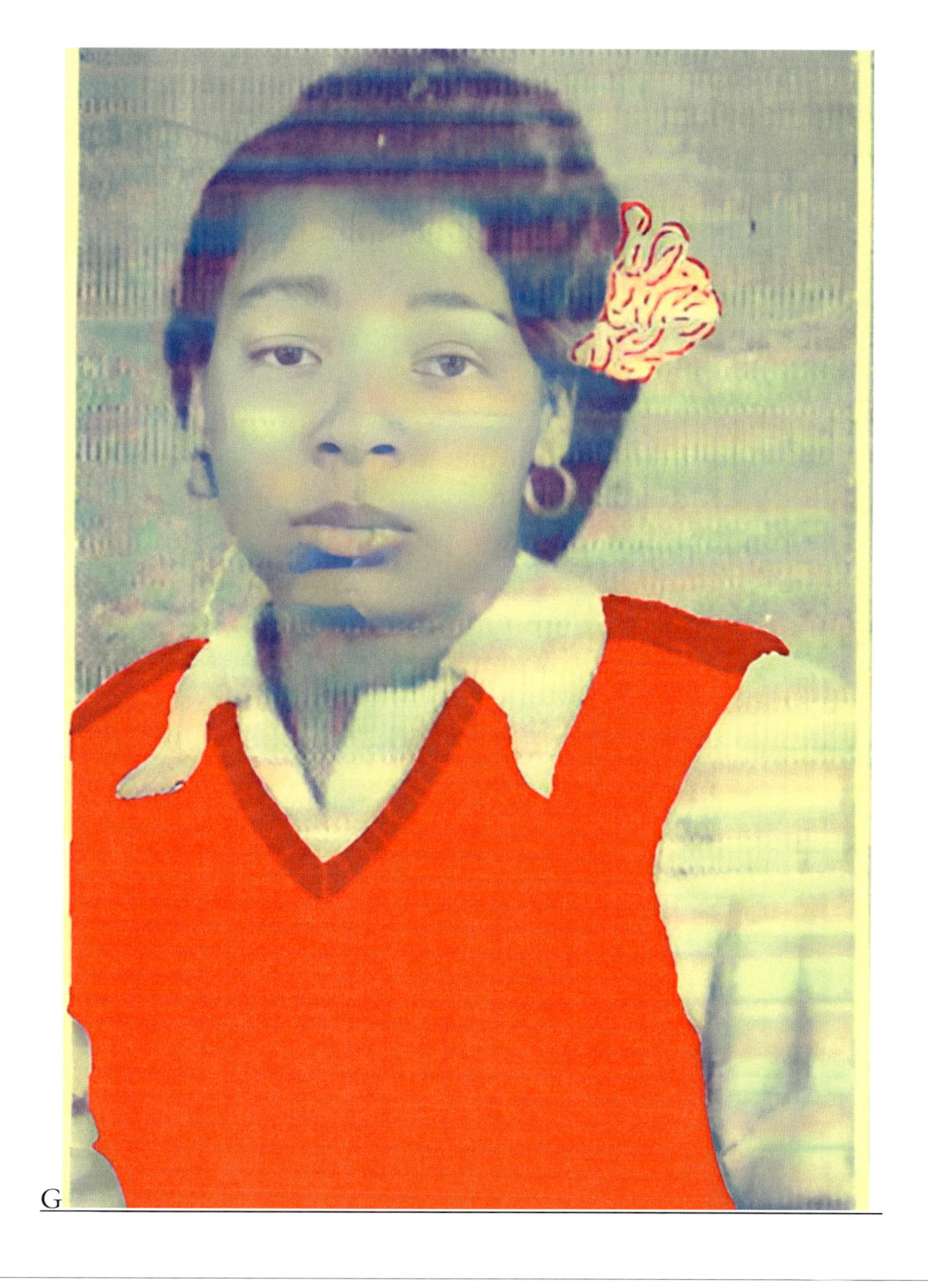

G

I married my first husband at 16. In my youthful innocence, I thought this would be a solution to not being able to stay out late but also to the local café. A good reason to marry, right? I don't even know why I thought I should stay out late, but this was my solution. It was a secret from my parents for two weeks. We got married on Saturday, and it hurt my parents when they found out. The following Sunday, I asked my new husband for a quarter for an ice cream cone; he didn't have it, so I asked my dad, and he said no, you got a husband. I knew I made a huge mistake.

Lula Mae Rogers

I walked around the neighborhood and saw a beauty shop called Two Sisters on a corner, so I went in to get a job; her name was Lula Mae Rodgers, she said. Baby, where is your mother? I told her I lived with my husband. She said how old are you? I told her I was 19, and she said I was to be. I want you to be your mama; I was so happy. A few years later, she married a man named Raymond Ross he didn't have any children either, so I became their child. Daddy Raymond opened a grocery store on the corner of Woods and Washington. We were on the west side, and eventually, I went to work for him.

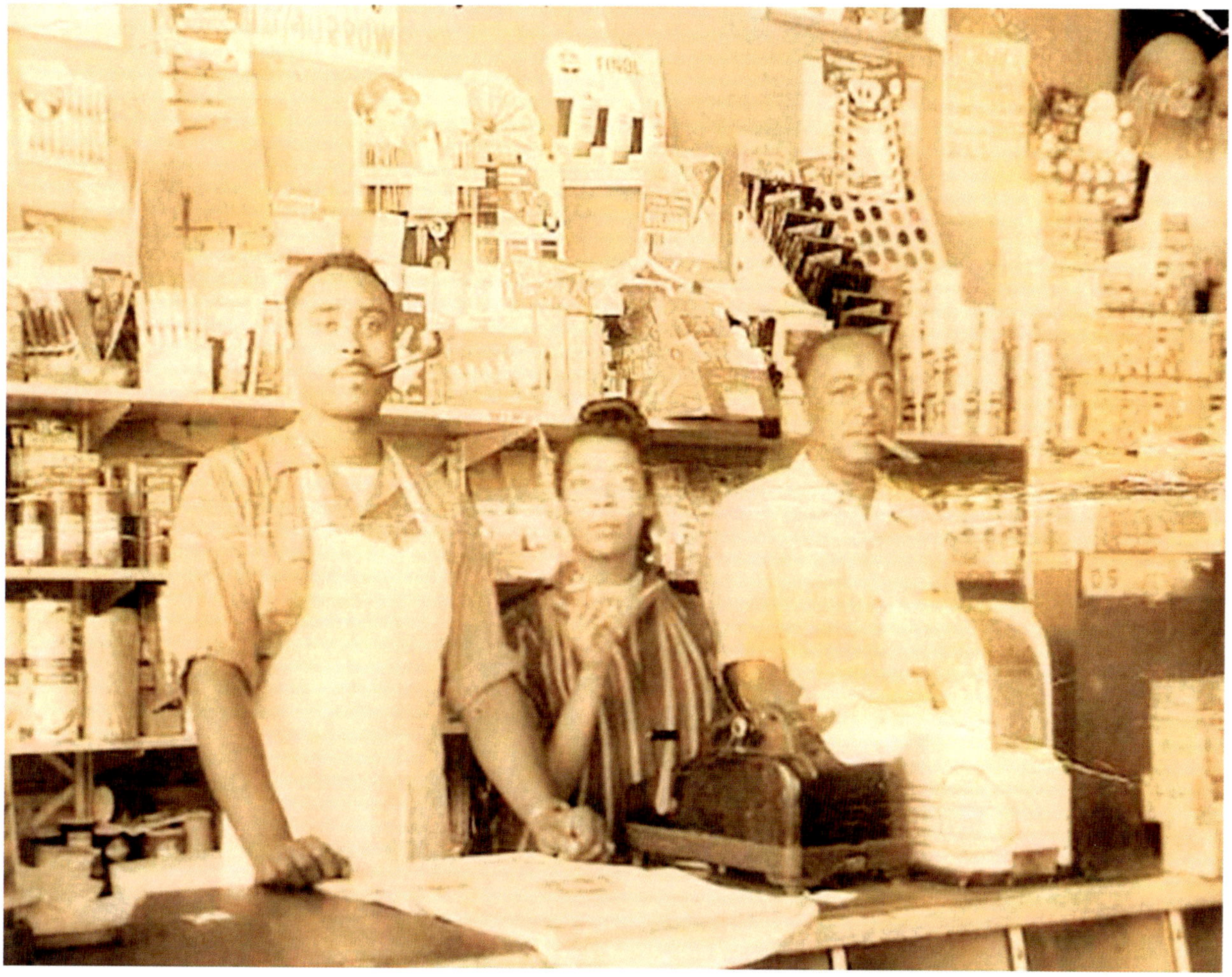

Separated but still married, I lived with a lady named Mrs. Chapman. I had friends in the apartment complex. Mercedes, Howard, Louise, and Virginia cared for me when I needed anything. I returned to my husband, thinking everything was good between us, but the landlord told me that a woman had been coming to the apartment. I knocked on the door before entering, and Raymond went to the door; he would not let me in, so I got a brick and broke the window out; he came out then but refused to let me in. Well, I called the police and told them he hit me, they believed me and took him to jail. I put all his clothes in the tub and poured bleach over them. I called a man named Taylor to take my clothes and furniture to my new house. We became friends even though I was nine months pregnant. He and his brother owned a pool table joint. I called my mother, and she came and stayed with me until Diane was born. Raymond visited me several times, but my new mom and dad were also around. I wanted a larger place, so I would go over to my girlfriend, Thelma Bridges, asking her to keep Diane so I could go up and down the blocks looking for a place.

It was a Sunday, and I found a lady who rented me a place at 2820 Washington Boulevard for 12 dollars a week. It was a 2-and-a-half-room kitchenette, me and my little girl. I got up and got her dressed. Diane was built like a little woman. I took her to my grocery store with me every day. Lots of people wanted to keep her. She was so cute and still is. Raymond opened a grocery store for me at 1228 South Woods I, where I sold groceries, beer, and ice cream to the neighborhood. My mom walked away and could not take it anymore; she and Daddy Raymond had marital troubles and separated.

They gave me a life outside Malvern; they loved me and my child. God sent them, and now my mother and daddy were in Arkansas, praying that I would be okay. I loved them both and loved them until they left this world. My dad was an alcoholic. He liked a young girl; her family would come into the store and get groceries for free. Her name was Christine. This bewilders me; my parents in Arkansas had a different lifestyle and temperament. Yet I did not judge Raymond and supported my Chicago mom when she married again and then again. She never had any children; she told me of the time she was pregnant, and I am not sure which husband it was for. But she said when it was time for the baby to come, it was a stillbirth. She said it was a girl, and she put her in a shoebox and buried her.

I cried when she left the room thanking God that he chose me to be her daughter. Daddy Raymond and I remained close as a father and daughter after he and Big Ma divorced. A singing group was in town one night, and we girls wanted to go.

I asked Dad to take me to the club. When he arrived at the club, the line was so long that he decided to take us to another club he was more familiar with on Roosevelt Road. This was a divine move, a life-changing decision for me. As he drove away, he admonished me not to forget to open the store in the morning. We walked into the club; it was filled with people. Since I worked nights, I was sleepy. After we had been there for a while, a young man came over and asked me if he brought someone to meet me. Would I wake up? I said yes, thinking he would bring somebody having difficulty getting a date. By contrast, he brought over this tall, gorgeous man with long eyelashes, big eyes, and curly hair, and I woke up immediately.

I got up enough nerve to ask him if he would take me home so the other girls could stay. He said yes, his name was Joe Cameron, and we started to see each other. I could not believe this handsome man would look at me. I had extremely low self-esteem, and I did not know why men were always attracted to me. We had been together for six months, and he wanted to move in, but I said no. I had the flu, and my mother came from Arkansas to stay with me. When she left for Arkansas, she took Diane back with her. Diane was about three years old. Joe asked to marry me, but I had first to get a divorce. I called my husband and asked him for a divorce. He wouldn't make it easy for me to get one, but I got it. When I wanted to be fancy, I would put my hair in an upsweep.

Married Life

My son looks just like his father. This is precisely how he looked that night in the club: curly black hair, puppy-dog eyes, and eyelashes that framed his beautiful brown eyes. 532 E. 87th Place was a wonderland of great memories. If you are a young parent with young children, cherish them because they grow up fast.

What I wouldn't give to be at my former home around Christmas Eve as my little ones anticipated the arrival of Santa Claus.

Back to my story: I wanted Joe to meet my daughter, so we met Diane in Arkansas. I didn't bring her back, but she would come later. Mother wanted her to stay so I could settle in with my new husband. From day one, he gave me his payday check and never missed a week bringing it to me. I saved for a down payment on our first house, so we got my baby Diane from my mother. Tonya was born in 1957 when we moved into our new home. In March 1961, Bonita was born, Michael was born in 1965, and Barbara was born in 1964.

We had a happy family. My home was in a neighborhood where everybody knew everyone. Diane had her first bike on the Block at age seven and her first car at age 16. It lasted six months. We had a happy life for 29 years. He was a hard-working man who provided for his family and never brought a suit, only standard work clothes.

I wore moo moos; my children came first. I joined Saint Mark's Methodist Church, and my kids were raised in church.

They went to Catholic schools, which I thought was best for them. Tonya didn't want to go to Catholic school, so I sent her to Lindblom, a good school; Diane went to Harlan, a good school.

Loss

My husband died in 1984. I had a tough time dealing with his death and suffered PTSD. Bonita and I found him drawing his last breath. I had just come in from a catering job. As of 2024, I have been a widow for 40 years. I moved to Arkansas the same year at the suggestion of my sister Latora. My mind was so fragile, and I wasn't thinking straight and developed depression. I was not accepted in the small town of my birth; the baby that my father so celebrated had lost her standing. They say you cannot go home again, well you can –just don't expect it to be the same. I longed for companionship and needed my friends; some came down to see me, and I will never forget them for that act of love. If I could advise anyone who is going through grief, it would be: do not go anywhere right away. You must go through the process of grief; there is no time frame in which to get through it.

The main thing to know is this: wherever you go, there you are, the same person, just in a different place.

Moving did not lessen the pain; it intensified because now I had to do it mostly alone. My daughter Bonita came with me to Arkansas. She found work in the financial world and was very successful.

She would come in from work every day, and I would look sad or have been crying. Each day, she would come through the door to me crying.

One day, she came in the door, looked at me, and said Mama, go home! It was nothing but a word; she bought me a nice Nissan Maxima. I called my son to drive me back to Chicago. I threw some clothes into a suitcase and returned to a warm welcome. My friends greeted me, my pastor, and my church welcomed me. I found a house on 10954 South Normal. Bonita helped me lay it out and returned to Little Rock.

When I got back from Arkansas, I started meeting men. One of them brought his daughter, Tiffany Smith. I saw her; she looked so sweet. I hugged her, and she felt my love. Her mother died when she was two years old, so I became a mother to her and her sister, Karla. They became my daughters, so now I have seven children.

Lucille's Poetry & Remembrances

I would often be inspired to jot down my thoughts at the most unconventional and random times, such as doing laundry, pin-curling my hair, or shopping for groceries at the Hi-Lo grocery store up on 87th in Chatham with my good friend Fran; she lived across the street. Fran and I were best buds; we both had a house full of children, so working full-time was impractical.

Being home with my children was my priority. I wanted to know how their day went when they came home from school and ensure they came home happy. Still, my passion for writing remained strong. I imagined being part of a panel of mentors whose writings would give advice, counsel, or encourage someone going through a hard time.

The following piece, which I named Speeches, was "born" after doing the dinner dishes. From out of nowhere, the piece interrupted my plans to sit down and watch the evening news; it came as no surprise, as all my life, I have been compelled to capture my sentiments on whatever was available. Thanks to my five school-aged children, it was usually notebook paper.

So, without a computer, a proper writing tablet or any other devices writers use today, the collection of unnamed pages inked in longhand on notebook paper is finally being published.

<u>Speeches</u>

Our speeches should aim to improve our voices' articulation. Our goal should be to become more fluent and gain confidence and poise. We strengthen our personalities by delivering speeches effectively, working efficiently with small groups, organizing our ideas more logically, and improving our s vocabulary.

When giving a message, it is essential to remember that the listener pays attention to each word, as all eyes are on us.

<u>Ode to God</u>

I thank my God. He granted me life, gave me love, and made me happy through many years of strife and sacrifices. Through his example, the right way will always suffice. The world can be cruel, grieving, and heartbreaking to live each day.

So, I am happy with joy. I never knew to see the smile on your face. I'll always thank God for blessing me with happiness I didn't expect.

Thank you, thank you, for a heart aching through a whole life worth living through. Growing up struggling, sacrificing laughter, crying, and loving life through its years of Joy and Pain, wasn't it worth it?

Life

Life, how sweet It is! I love life. I love all the happiness that comes from above. Thanks to God for all. Love, there is no limit to my blessings; there are so many beautiful things to behold. Life is so precious. Like silver and gold, like Silk and wool, there is God. My God is always with me, excellent and bad, happy and sad, rich and poor. His goodness consumes me. I am blessed. Life is short. Life is long; life is a journey, making the best of it as a chore, not knowing that no matter what it is, we all want more, so come what may. I'm glad I'm here. Thank you, God, for giving me life and making it complete.

Life Is Like Sand

Little man with a bucket of sand, play outside as long as you can. Soon, the rain will wash away the sand, and you won't find Little Man.

Old Lady, Old Lady

Old lady, old lady, what took you so long? We were waiting and watching for you to come home. We have Millie, Doris, and Lily. Willie Mae looks so beautiful here. I see people, and they all ask about you and what I can say daily. Old lady, be on your way, right?

The Necessary Part

I am happy because you have become a necessary part of my life. I have never known a more peaceful part. When did I know who you are? You make me happy and cry; why don't I walk and say goodbye because you fulfill me in every way? I can't deny myself; oh, Sorrows, why? So where? Who am I? When am I? Why am I? I'm yours. I love you, long trips, short trips, nice trips, bad trips, happy trips, and trips getting away from home for a while. Good Times, bad times, crazy times, sad times, oh how it would be to get a vacation from home from kids, from a job, from the cares of the world.

Thoughts

Life is short. Life is long, a journey, and making the best of it is a chore. We matter. What it is we all want more. So, come. What? May I'm glad I'm here. Thank you for granting me life and making it full of little strife. I give thanks.

Prayer

There are so many wonders to be found day in and day out. Life is so precious, like silver, gold, Silk, and wool. There is good and evil, happy and sad, rich and poor. My God is always with me. His goodness consumes me.

Love Question

Why do I? When didn't I? Who are you? What don't I? Whose am I? Where could I? You are the answer. You are the reason you make me happy. You make me sad. Why don't I walk away? And say goodbye. Just because you fulfill me in every way, I can't deny myself of Sorrows. That's why, so where, when, what, who am I, and why am I totally in? I don't know, I love you!

The Raven

One of my favorite poetry recitations is Edgar Allen Poe's *The Raven*. I memorized every verse. She was so impressed with my speaking voice and ability to recite poetry and short stories that she wanted me to travel and teach with her.

I backed out at the last minute and wondered how my life would have turned out had I accepted the offer. However, I do not regret the path God has led me down.

I was always the leader they could admire. Childhood squabbles and arguments sometimes surface without warning, and I often wonder if I could have said or done something better to be there for them while seeking my ambition.

We can all reflect on our humanism and say, "I wish I could have. I hope they know that I love and miss them. Even if we didn't talk daily, I knew they were there and was happy to speak to them whenever possible. Sadly, that is no longer the case. My brother Titus served in the military, and after he had fulfilled his tenure, he moved to California and married a beautiful young lady named Billie. They have one son, whom we affectionately call Tyke. My sister Lillian was very musically inclined. She played the piano for her church and worked at the state hospital in Benton. Lillian married Herbert Beard and had three daughters and one son, Melba, Marion, Barbara, and Herbert, Jr. Melba loved to wear my clothes; when she would visit me in Chicago, she would try on everything in my closet and leave it on the bed. I didn't care, though; I was happy to see her and pleased that she was enjoying herself. Barbara is an accomplished nurse and lives in California. She never forgets my birthday or Mother's Day. I can always receive a box from her on those two occasions.

Marion has an activist spirit, too. She is a community organizer, oversees the Henson Benson Foundation, and has run several political offices in Malvern. Her son, Herbert, is a hardworking man who loves his wife and children and is a great provider. In December 1983, tragedy knocked on the door of the Smith family. Two weeks before Christmas Eve, we lost Melba. She would be one of many for our family who were called home to be with the Lord before they could make their mark on this earth.

I know God is too good to make mistakes. My sister Latora had three sons and one daughter, Donna. I did not see my nephews as much as I wanted to, but I did get to visit with Donna and Latora often. Donna is married to a wonderful man named Marvin, and they have two sons. Her three brothers and a niece, Toni, have all gone home to be with the Lord. It's funny how we grow up, start our families, and grow apart from many people to whom we were so close. I don't think it is anything deliberate. Life works that way. You pay intricate attention to your immediate family and the issues that matter to them, and eventually, you are so engaged that it is all you can do to keep up with them. It was years before I gained a social life. I always wanted to be available for my children, but as they got older, I joined two social clubs: the Lovely Ladies and the Juniors.

Life is like the four Seasons. In the summer of our youth, we spend our early years trying to find purpose. We enter our spring season with determination and an agenda for life, and our choices become wiser and more metered, heading toward our chosen pathways. It's usually at this time of our lives that we seek something greater than ourselves. Most of us find it in Jesus Christ, but not all. In our fall, we are older, carrying the regrets and scars gained along the way. There are disappointments, losses, and rebounds, and in our winter season, there is a settling. Because we know that there are more years behind us than ahead. We want our lives to matter; we need to leave a legacy.

We want to be remembered as someone who tried to make life better for all we encountered. In our humanity, we may have more losses than wins. Where is our deliverer who can give us a life of peace, right our wrongs, and reconcile us back to God? The Apostle Paul said in Romans 7:24, "Who will rescue me from this body that is subject to death?" He said: "Thanks be to God, who delivers me through Jesus Christ our Lord!" The deliverance from sin and death comes through faith in Jesus Christ and the indwelling presence of the Holy Spirit. Jesus looks past our mistakes or sins and covers them with his blood so we become God's righteousness in Christ Jesus. I have been writing down little passages of my life and sharing them openly with you—unashamed. God has taken me on a journey where I can look back and say that, too, has passed. I want to leave a legacy for my children, family, loved ones, and those who know me. Lucille could cook, was passionate and compassionate, and loved her children and family. I may not remember everything about my past, but I am sure of my future. "For the Lord himself shall descend from heaven with a shout, with the voice of the archangel, and with the trump of God: and the dead in Christ shall rise first:" 1 Thessalonians 4:6. I'm ready!

My Favorite Recipes

This isn't a traditional cookbook; I pray it will be passed down to each generation to come. I hope these dishes become a family tradition collection, as they are some of my favorite recipes. I have served them at parties, weddings, events, birthday parties, etc. I have named a unique recipe for each of my seven children.

CHICKEN SALAD CAKE

8 cups of chicken salad

Large round tray

Place chicken mixture on the tray

Make the shape of a layer of cake.

Add another mix for another layer on top.

And one more cake-shaped mixture until you have three layers and…

The chicken salad looks like a cake.

Take cream cheese and mix it with the food coloring of choice.

Take a spatula and spread cream cheese like icing like icing a cake

Do it smoothly, and make sure each layer is a different size

Use cherry tomatoes, pimentos, cream cheese, and a few corn kernels for the top of the cake, use your imagination.

FRUIT EXPLOSION

Use grapes, orange wedges, cherries, apples

strawberries, kiwi, and blackberries

Arrange the fruit in random sections on the tray as pictured

Then, on the front and back, and top.

Place small Bundles of grapes and melons.

SOUTHERN SMOTHERED LIVER W ONIONS

This recipe is dedicated to my son Michael.

Please liver on a tray

Sprinkle seasoned salt and flour on both sides

Brown both sides and heat the oven

Cut up onions and water to make gravy and

Finish cooking slowly, stirring,

Place it in the oven.

At 350 degrees until done about 40 minutes

TASTY STRING BEANS WITH POTATOES

Use One gallon of store or Commercial-style green beans

Pour out water and put fresh water in a large pot and the meat of choice

Put on the stove on low to 200 degrees

Simmer on low all night

Turn it off in the morning.

Boil separately cut white potatoes and add to String Beans

Sprinkle Mrs. Dash on Potatoes

They taste fresh from the Garden Beans.

DELICIOUS BATTERED SHRIMP

Peel and devein medium to Jumbo shrimp

Use 1.5 cups of pancake mix

Add one egg and put in enough water to bind.

Mix and egg together, then add a can of beer, any brand

. It would be best to have the consistency to dip a shrimp in it, and it stays coated.

Put in a hot skillet (400) and fry until golden brown 5 – 7 minutes

You could also use mixed for broccoli, cauliflower, okra & meatballs

garnished with/ lemon

SAVORY ROAST BEEF STEW

This recipe is dedicated to my daughter Bonita.

Wash and pat dry. Make tiny pockets with a knife point.

Add a clove of garlic to each one of the pockets

Add Lowry seasoning salt and flour-coated

Brown on both sides, put it in a roasting pot, and slice onions.

Add carrots and potatoes

Place in oven at 250 degrees for 1 hour 45 minutes till tender.

Garnish with carrot strips, potatoes, and rosemary garnish.

DELICIOUS SOUTHERN FRIED PORK CHOPS

This recipe is dedicated to my daughter Barbara.

Wash Chops and pat Dry.

Rub dry seasoning of choice.

Add Lawry seasoned salt and flour.

Fry in hot oil until brown

Add 1 cup of water and simmer for 20 minutes to have a light gravy on the side.

Serve over rice or with mashed potatoes

Garnish with potatoes and parsley with basil

HOT WATER CORNBREAD

Boil 3 cups of water.

When water boils, remove from stove and 1.5 cups of cornmeal.

Stir with a spoon and pat into patties.

Run cold water in the sink.

Pat hot patties with cold water and Fry until golden brown.

If serving with greens/garnish with scallions

PEACH COBBLER

This recipe is dedicated to my daughter, Tiffany Smith

Purchase 2 long boxes of Pillsbury Brand Pie crust

Take out both rolls, take the wrapping off, and cut in one 1-inch strips

Place in an aluminum pan.

Roll out six strips until Brown.

Take out of the oven and add two large cans of peaches

add 2 cups of sugar

Sprinkle two large tablespoons of flour

Sprinkle 1 tbsp of nutmeg and one stick of butter.

Take the remaining two rolls, cut them into 1-inch strips, and crisscross

Bake until Brown at 350 for 45 minutes

SOUTHERN COOKED COLLARD GREENS

Two bags of fresh collard greens

Open bags, Wash greens, and throw away the big stems.

Put greens in a pot with five cups of already boiling water

Season with meat to your taste

Add Green Pepper Strips

Add salt, pepper, garlic, three shakes of hot sauce, and three tablespoons of sugar.

Put in a pot of boiling water with the meat of choice.

I use salt pork or turkey tails.

It is best if cooked overnight on low.

LOUISIANA HOT FRIED FISH

Use about 10 – 15 Fresh fish fillets

Rinse fish and pat dry

Use Old and Bay, a small amount of Lawry's

Coat both sides with cornmeal/flour mixture (1/2 0f each)

Put in hot oil, about 375 to 400

Fry for approximately 7 minutes on each side

BROWN SUGAR GLAZED BAKED HAM

Wash 5-pound ham

Season to taste

Add pineapples/cherries with toothpicks

Make Glaze with Brown Sugar and Ginger ale

Add cherries and pineapples as pictured

Pour Ginger ale with Brown Sugar on top

Bake at 350 for 1 ½ hours

SOUTHERN CORNBREAD DRESSING

THIS RECIPE IS DEDICATED TO MY DAUGHTER TONIA
Two cups of cornbread have everything in it.
add 2 cups of milk and one egg
poured into a greased Skillet and cook at 350 until Brown
Take it out, place it into a large pan, and
Add four slices of white toast
Cut up three stalks of celery and a large onion
Cut up one can of cream chicken soup.
Rinse the can with water twice,
and add one package of dry onion soup mix
and one tablespoon of poultry seasoning.
put your chicken on top.
cover it with aluminum foil for 1 hour until done.
Buy one package of brown gravy mix.
Put oil and skillet, add flour, stir, and water, stir until thick, like gravy,
and slice boiled eggs and serve as the gravy for the dressing

THIS RECIPE IS DEDICATED TO MY DAUGHTER KARLA
SOUTHERN STYLE RUTABAGAS

Cut whole rutabagas in half only then

Peel cut up in chunks

The meat of your choice, cook for 45 minutes or on top of the stove

Add salt or Lawry Seasoning salt if needed.

CREAMY CHEESY MACARONI & CHEESE

Macaroni and cheese boil water for 7 minutes

Remove from the stove and put in sink in the cold-water

Run in the pot until cloudy water turns clear.

Start with an aluminum pan or whatever you choose.

Add a cup of milk

Add water to it and add Lawry-seasoned

Add one egg and a layer of macaroni

and then cheese, then at least one layer of cheese on top

Cut a stick of butter on top and place it in the oven at 350 for 35 minutes.

GOODY GOODY GUMBO

Boil chicken and water in a large pot to start cooking.

While you prepare the other ingredients, cut up three stalks of celery,

Two layers of onions and two cloves of garlic.

And green pepper sauté and set aside next, start your roux

1 cup of oil and 1 cup of flour stir slowly

Please do not go away from the stove

Continue to stir until it starts to look like peanut butter

Set it aside, cut up gumbo sausage, or

The closest you can get to spicy soft sausages

If the chicken is done, add all cooked ingredients,

Then, add four blue crabs and crab legs,

and use gumbo spices to taste

If you want okra, cut it into pieces.

TASTY CANDIED SWEET POTATOES

Add to a large skillet or a heavy pan.
Of water halfway to the top
add a cup of ½ of sugar.
Cut four sweet potatoes into slices, about 4 or 5 slices into a pot
When sugar and water start to boil, add the potatoes
Cook until the potatoes turn orange as transparency remains.
Add more potatoes you have cooked in the water and nutmeg to the syrup water
All the potatoes are put in a pan, and one stick of butter is cut up.
Over the potatoes, pour the leftover cooked potatoes

FISH-SHAPED TUNA MOLD

Make the fish with two large cans of tuna

Mix mayonnaise pickles, relish, and celery.

Put it in a tray, take your hands,

and roll it into the shape of a fish.

Use cucumber fins on the tail

Put a red piece of tomato for his eyes or a pimento.

Mold mixture and shape of a fish and

Make scales of cucumbers sliced thin

CHICKEN FRICASSEE

Cut Up Chicken pieces

Wash chicken and pat dry

add Lawry's seasoning salt

Put flour on the chicken

Put chicken in bag and shake It well

Please put in the oven for 1 hour on 300 until it gets brown

BUTTERY FRIED YELLOW CORN

Put oil or butter in a skillet, add 1/3 cup of flour the flour

Add two cans of whole-kernel corn with water in them.

You can add seasonings and stir fry till creamy

Yummy!

THIS RECIPE IS DEDICATED TO MY DAUGHTER DIANE

GREEN PEPPER SPAGHETTI WITH SALSA-TOMATO SAUCE

Boil 16 oz of Spaghetti Noodles for 7 minutes

Drain and season with butter and a little salt and set aside

Sautee one chopped onion and one green pepper in butter

Ground 2 pounds ground sirloin season with Lawry's and black pepper

Drain meat and add sauté vegetables

Combine on large jar 32 ounces of preferred tomato sauce

Add one 12-ounce jar of mild salsa

Serve with Hot Garlic Bread and Green Salad – Scrumptious!!!!

Welcome to my life in photos

THE HERITAGE COLLECTION

Some of the most beloved family photos

Enjoy the walk down memory lane!

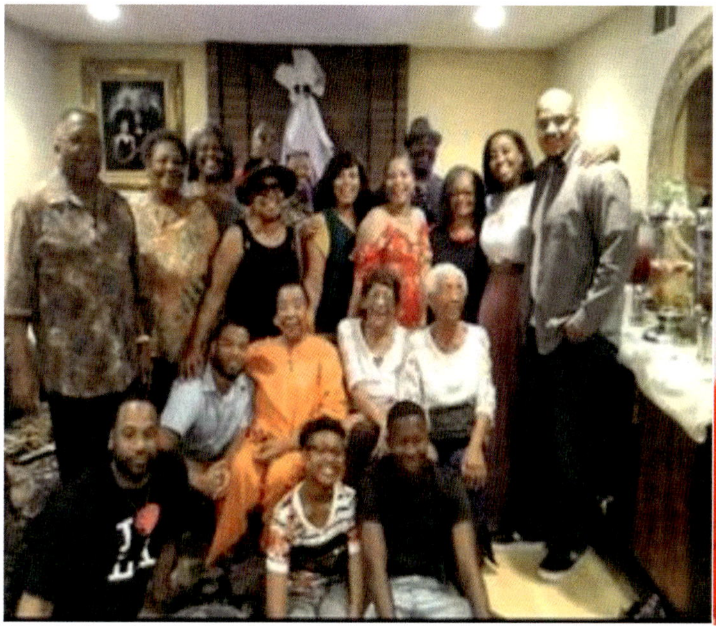

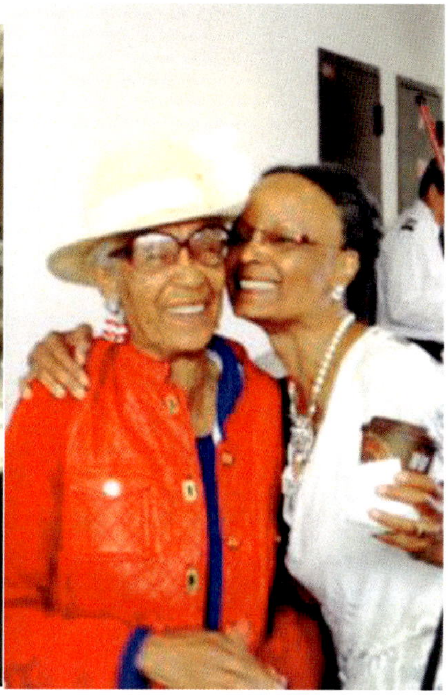

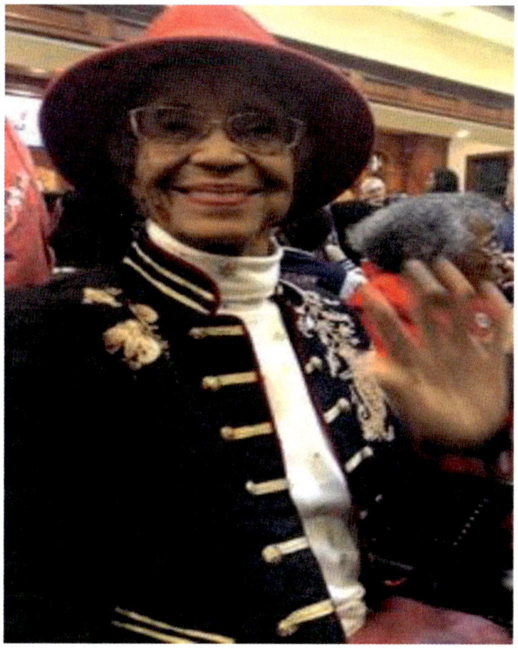

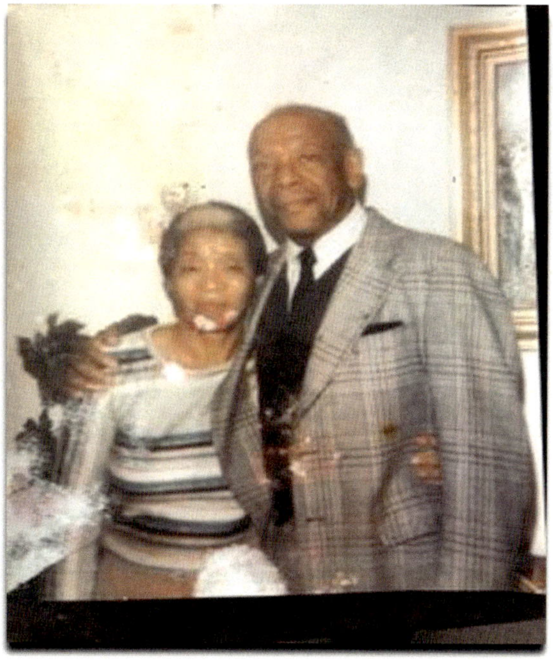

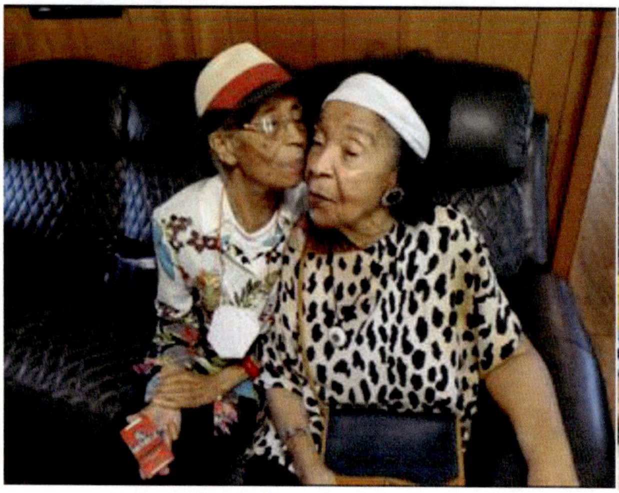

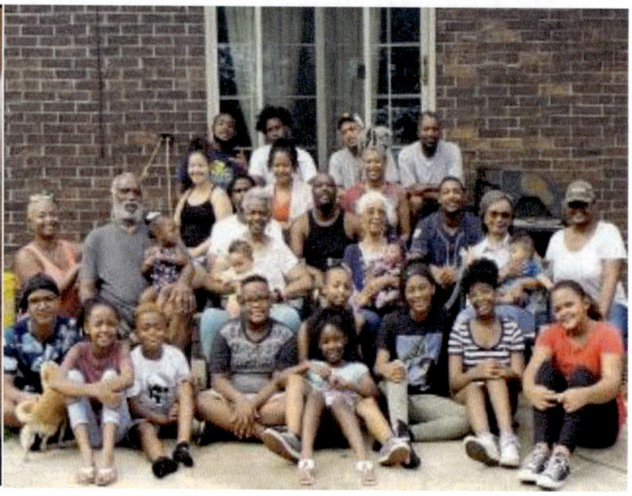

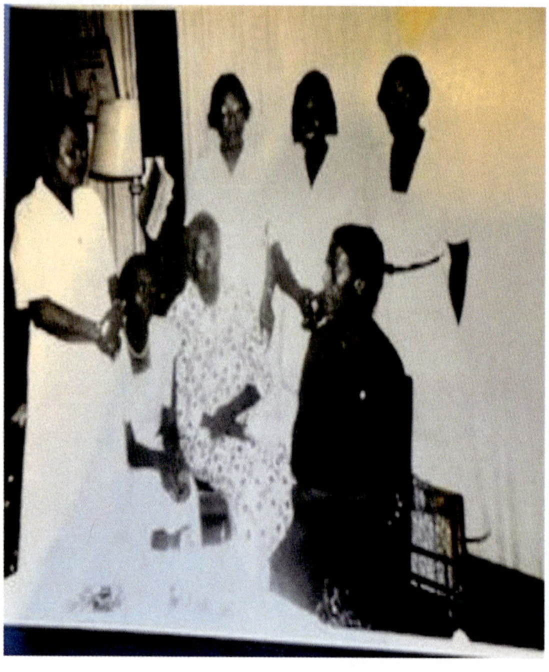

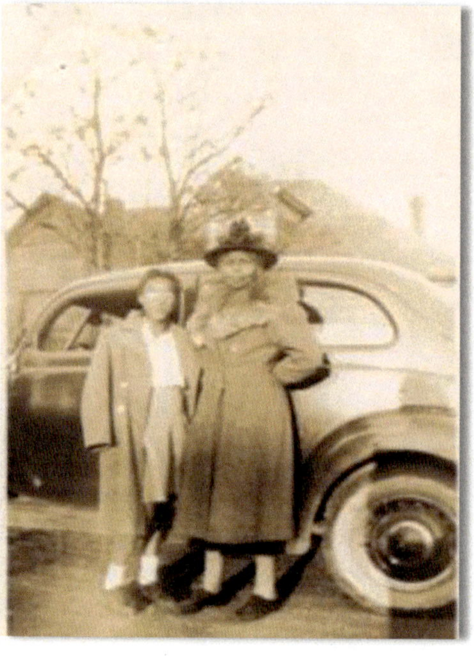

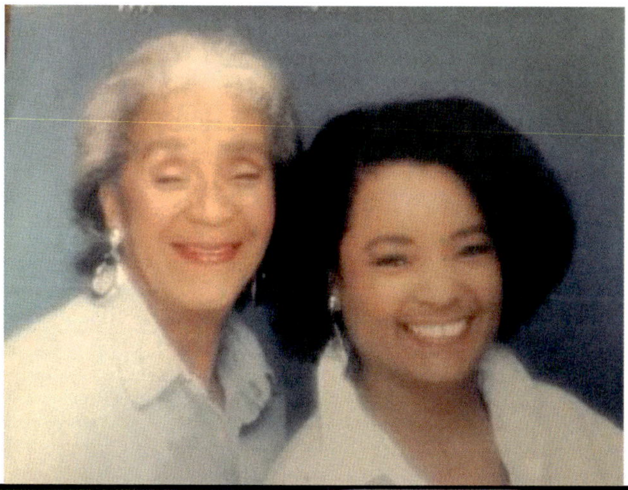

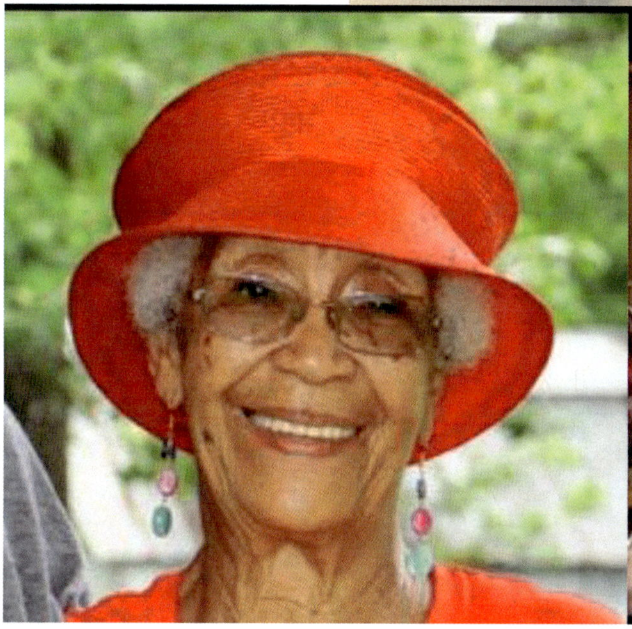

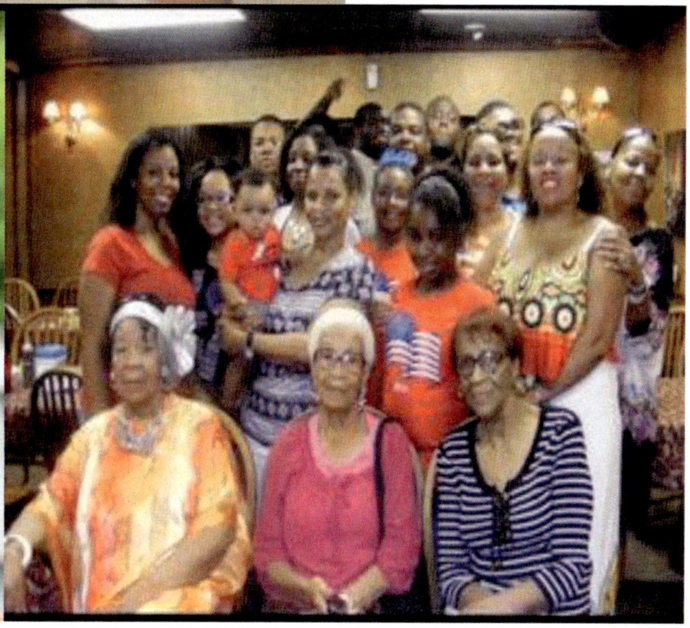

Lucille & and five of her seven children: l-r; Bonita, Diane, Lucille, Michael, Tonia, Barbara

Cousins Me and My Sisters Children, Granddaughters, and Daughter in Love

Our family in Los Angeles at the funeral of our only Brother, Titus
Lucille in White next to Billie (Rip), our late brother Titus's wife

Latora, Lucille, Titus, Lillian
I am the only one left, but I will see them again, God promised!

Smith Children and Aunt Verna

Sisters and Cousins

Easter Dinner with Mom and Dad in Arkansas

Mom, Regis, Bill (RIP) at Regis's graduation from Duke University

Sisters

Lucille and Barbara

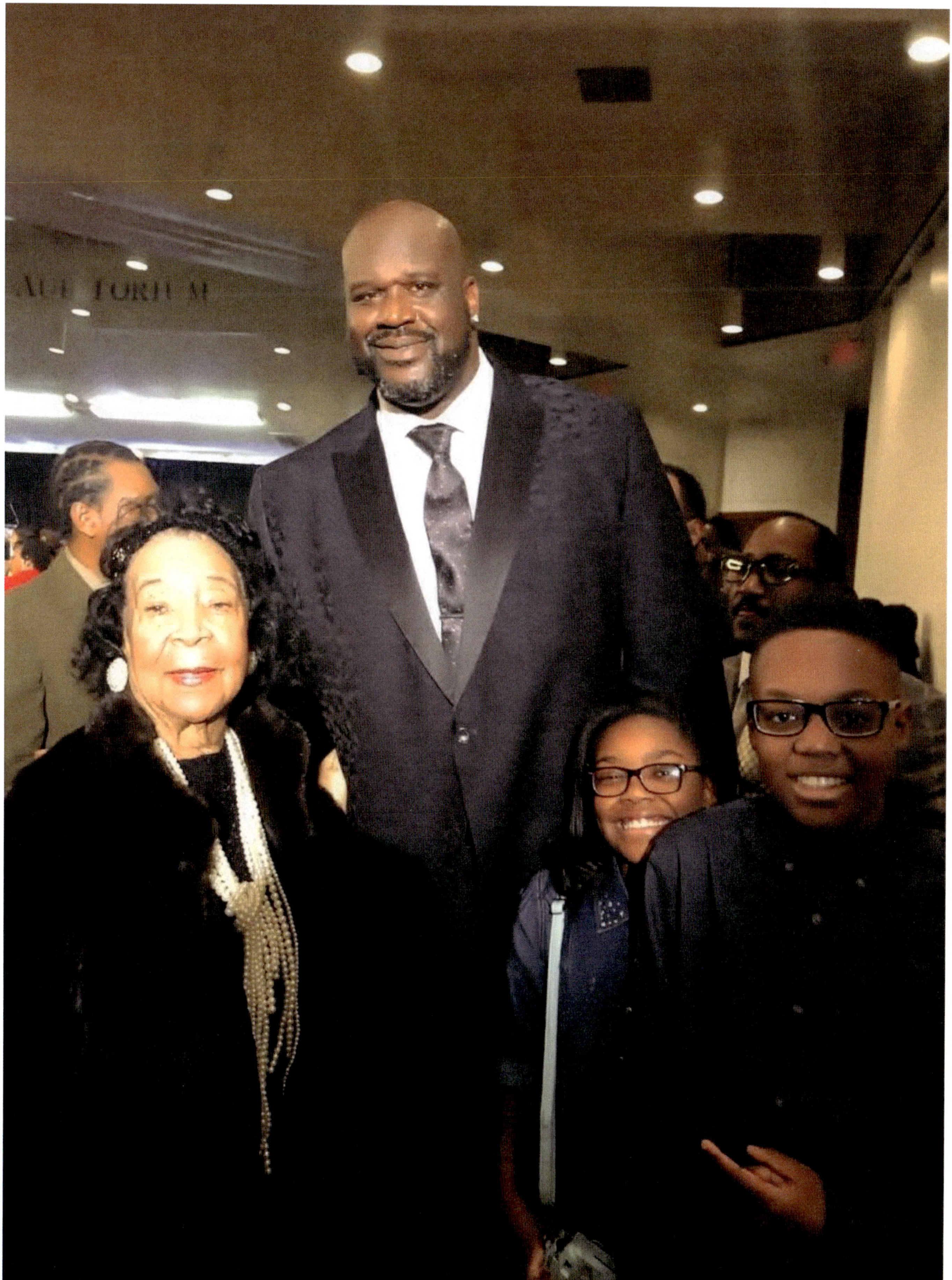

The Three Divas

Sophisticated Lucille

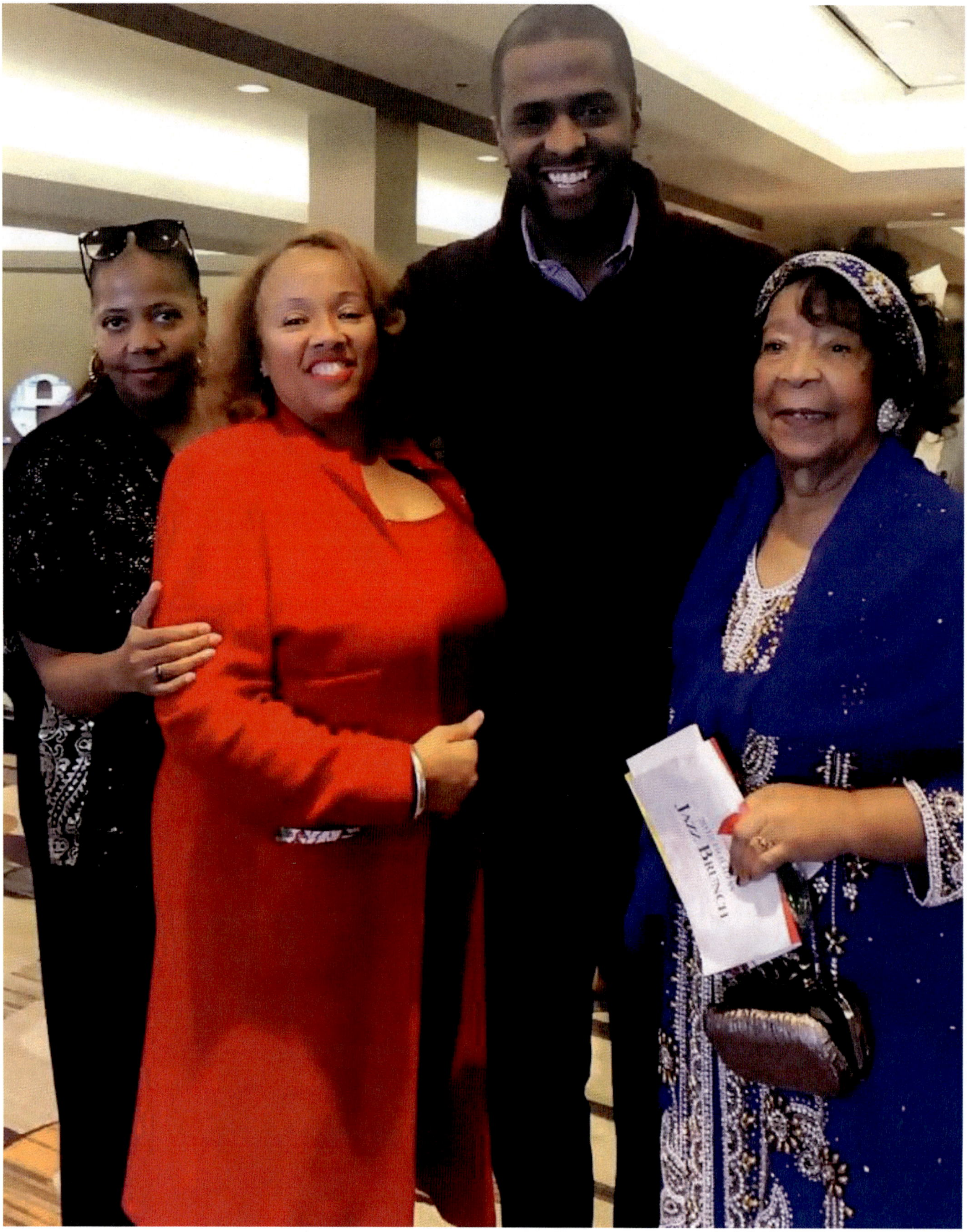
JAZZ BRUNCH

My Great Great Great Grandfather Isaac Smith... 1824 - 1909 - RIP Granddaddy, and thanks for paving the way!!
How often do we neglect to talk to our living family elders,
They are the real keepers of the treasures of our family history.

Sisters

Granddaughter Shehawnee

Diane with Mayor Omar Neal of Tuskegee and the Delegation from Africa
Lucillie met with them all

Bonita, Pastor Chester Jones & Lucille

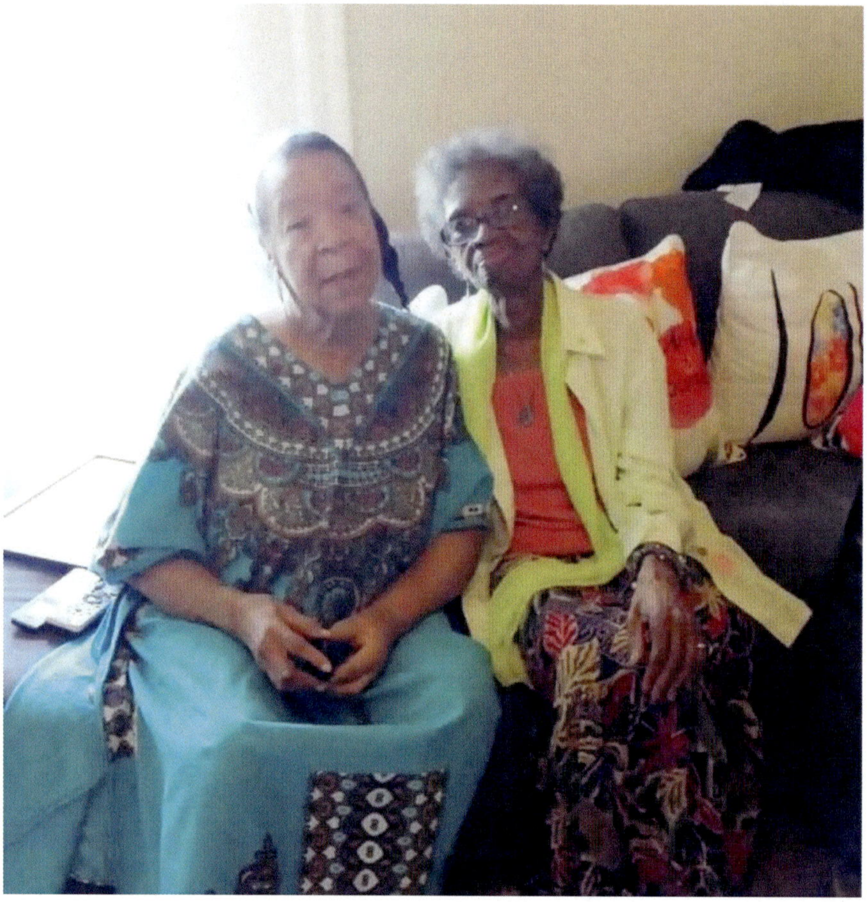

Big Baller Lucille in Vegas

Lucille and Lillian at Thanksgiving

Lucille in the Bahamas

Tonya, Michael, Lucille

Big Ben (RIP), Bo, Lucille

Uncle George Gloster. Gramma Louise Gloster's Brother.

Lucille & Pastor Williams

On the way to Church Service – Michael & Lucille

Lucille and Michael on the pier at Harbor Town, Hilton Head

Lucille & Micheal at Shelter Cove Harbor, Hilton Head

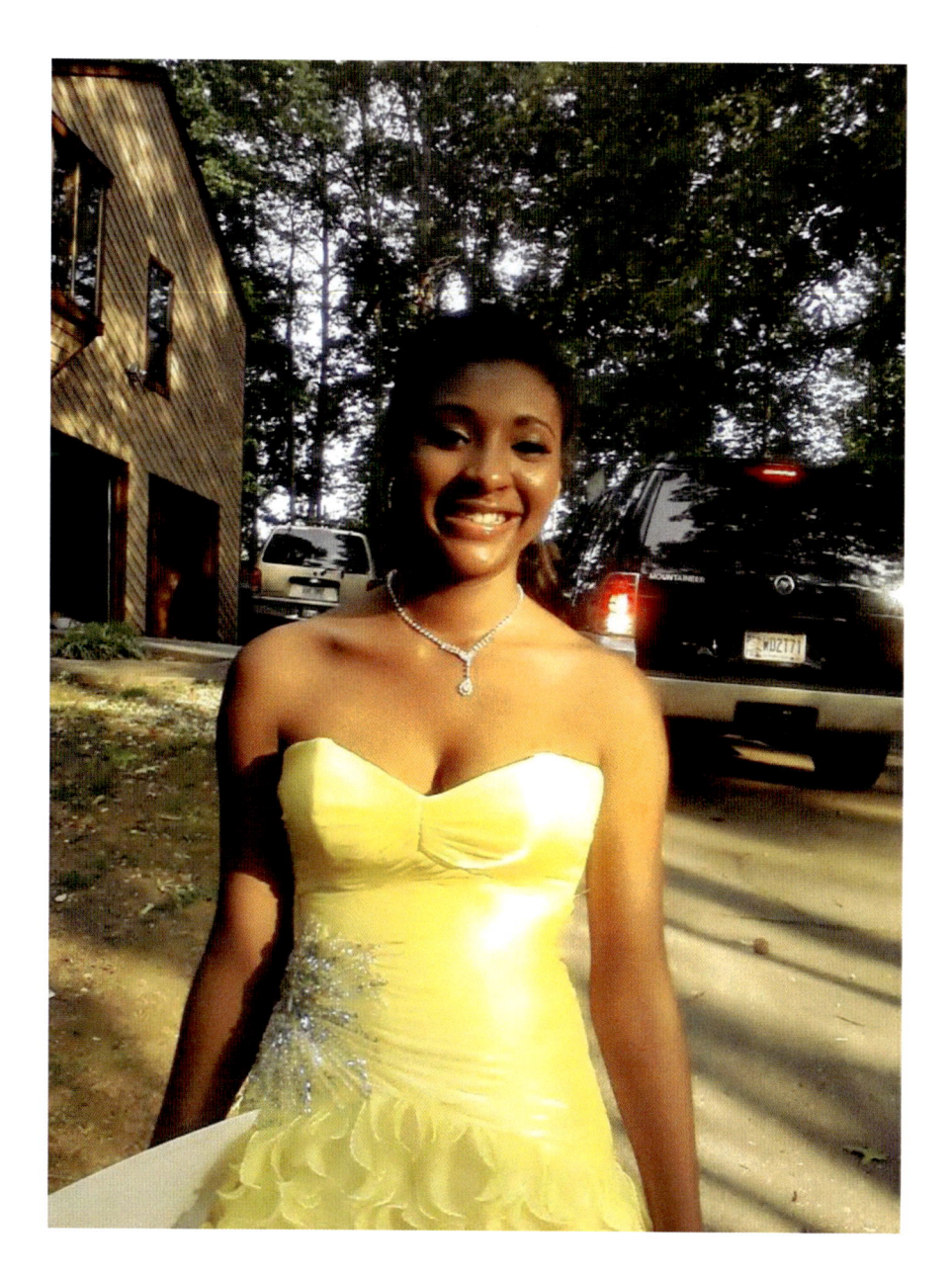

Taylor at the Prom

Lucille and her Bonus Son, Former Mayor Omar Neal
Of Tuskegee and his Lovely Family

Cousins, Herbert Beard & Michael Cameron

Joe & Lucille

Jaren Elam

EJ and Marina

Great Granddaughter of Lucille, Erin & Jarreau's Twins

Congratulations Erin & Jarreau

Two little cuties on the way!

The Baby Shower (Twins) Attendees

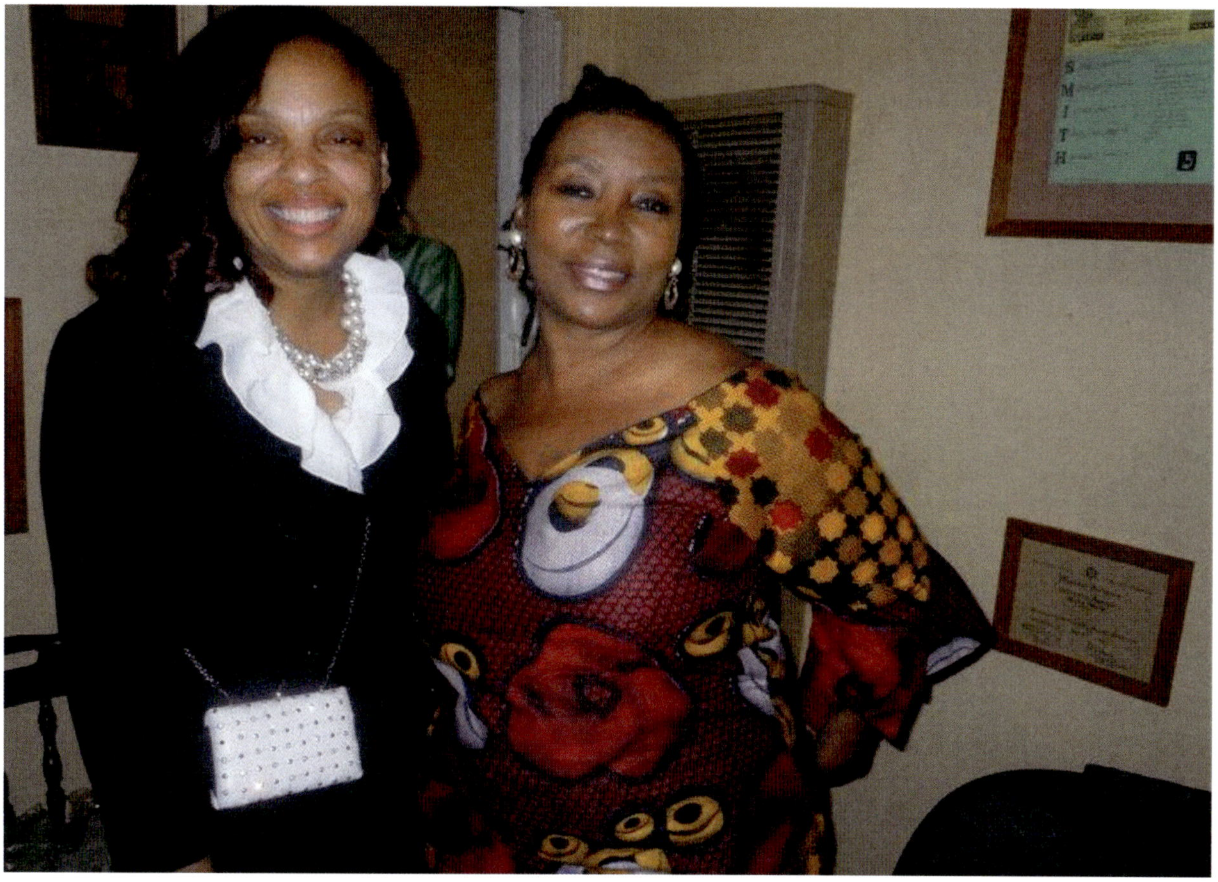
SMITH

2018 Malvern Wilson Reunion –
Chardonee & Herbert (Cousins)

Past Malvern Wilson Reunion

Cousins Ronnie & Ola Fay

Lillian proud of Grandson Jamal being featured in the paper

Tiffany and Mom (Lucille)

Family

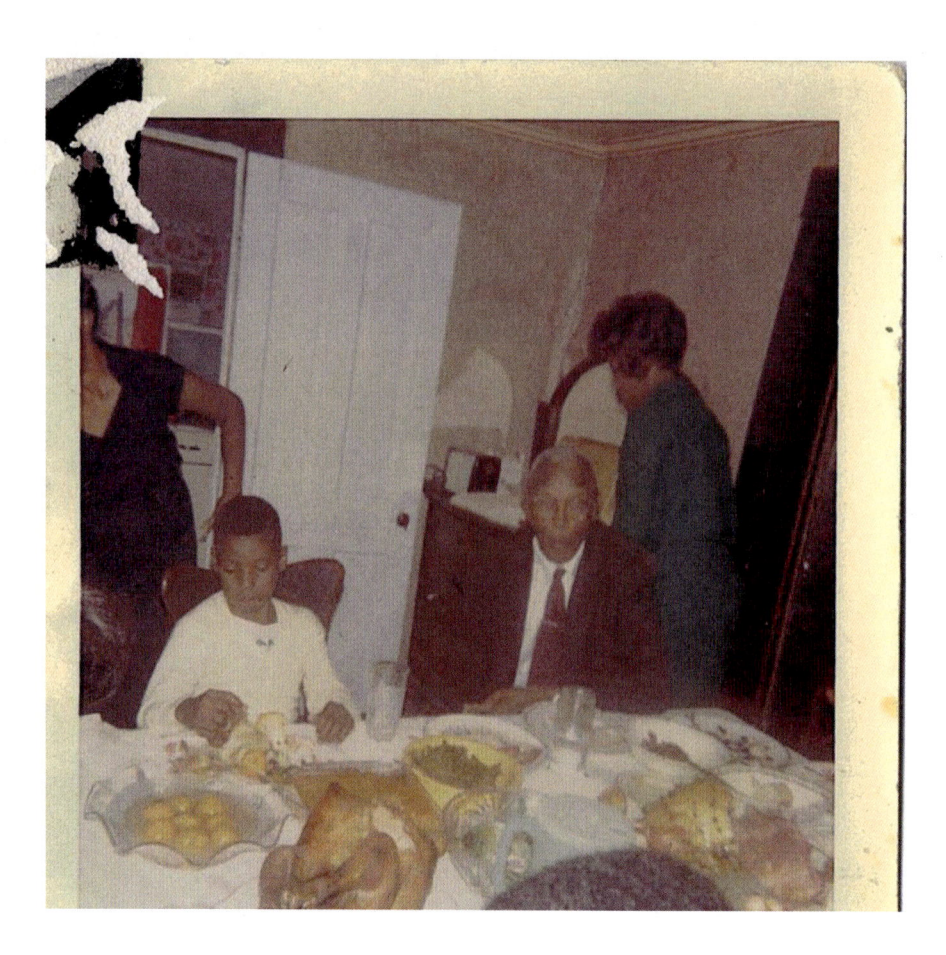

Thanksgiving at the Smith Home

Melba (Rest in Peace, My Love)

Donna & Marion

Marion Gibson
Henson Benson Foundation

By VIRGINIA PITTS
MDR Reporter

...c leader Marion Gibson was born ...ed in Malvern. She moved to ...California in adulthood and ... ... years there, where she moved to Arkansas in 1990 and resided here for about 12 years before moving to Kentucky.

Gibson's position as an extension agent and administrator with Kentucky State University, a historically black ... a tremendous impact in the black community there through various programs she managed, such as the vital work she did to reunite children in the foster system with their immediate families.

Gibson stated that families of color are represented at a higher rate in the child welfare and foster care system but underrepresented in terms of administration and law enforcement officials who work in that system. Many people of color are hesitant to go through the legal steps or the court process to regain custody because being surrounded by white judges, white lawyers, and white officials and cops, can sometimes feel like a hostile environment.

If the majority of the people in the system are black, and most of the people running the system are white, it seems like common sense that black people would feel contempt or mistrust for a system that can't relate. This simple fact is an issue Gibson was able to address with a presence and voice of understanding, and the means to affect change and help those families work through the proper channels and get out of the system for good.

Gibson moved back to the Malvern area after she retired from the university position. She decided to join with other concerned citizens to form the civic group "Malvern Citizens for Positive Change" when a local high school teacher made national news in late 2016 for posting racist comments about Michelle and Barak Obama on social media.

Pressure from this group, along with other local individuals and organizations, led to the teacher's resignation and a much-needed dialogue about people of color not being represented in proportion to the number of black teachers working in the school district. As a result, more teachers of color have been hired, and the civic group's efforts have extended throughout the community to combat social inequity in the workforce.

Gibson was the Outreach Manager for the 2020 Census and was instrumental in raising understanding of the census, its purpose, and the benefits of participating.

She currently serves on the ASU... Community Advisory Committee and the Baptist Health Hot Spring County Advisory Board.

She is secretary of the local Democratic National Committee chapter and worked on Joyce Elliot's 2020 campaign for U.S. House in Arkansas's 2nd congressional district.

She is also the current President of the Henson Benson Foundation, a local non-profit organization that provides scholarships and resources to high-achieving students of color in the area. The foundation strives to ... leadership skills and promote academic excellence, community improvement, and civic duty in the hearts and ... of the youth of Hot Spring County.

Gibson is working with other like-minded citizens who think ... ing alcohol sales to Hot Spring ... could be of great financial bene... want to get the "wet/dry" issue ... ballot so the people can decide ... themselves.

Gibson has been married ... Cornelius Gibson for 30 years ... blessed with four children ...

Marion, we are all proud of her

We love you, Mom, and are proud of your accomplishments.

May this be the first of many books that you write!!!!!

Love

Bonita

Karla

Tonia

Tiffany

Barbara

Diane

Michael

All the Grandchildren

Both the Great Grands

Your Family, Friends, and Special Friends,

Nieces, Nephews, Cousins

Bobby, Robert, Troy

Brother & Sister In-Laws, Pearl, Bruce, Bertha, Christine, Juana and

Children's Friends

My Milestone

Picture Memories

of

The 90th Birthday Party

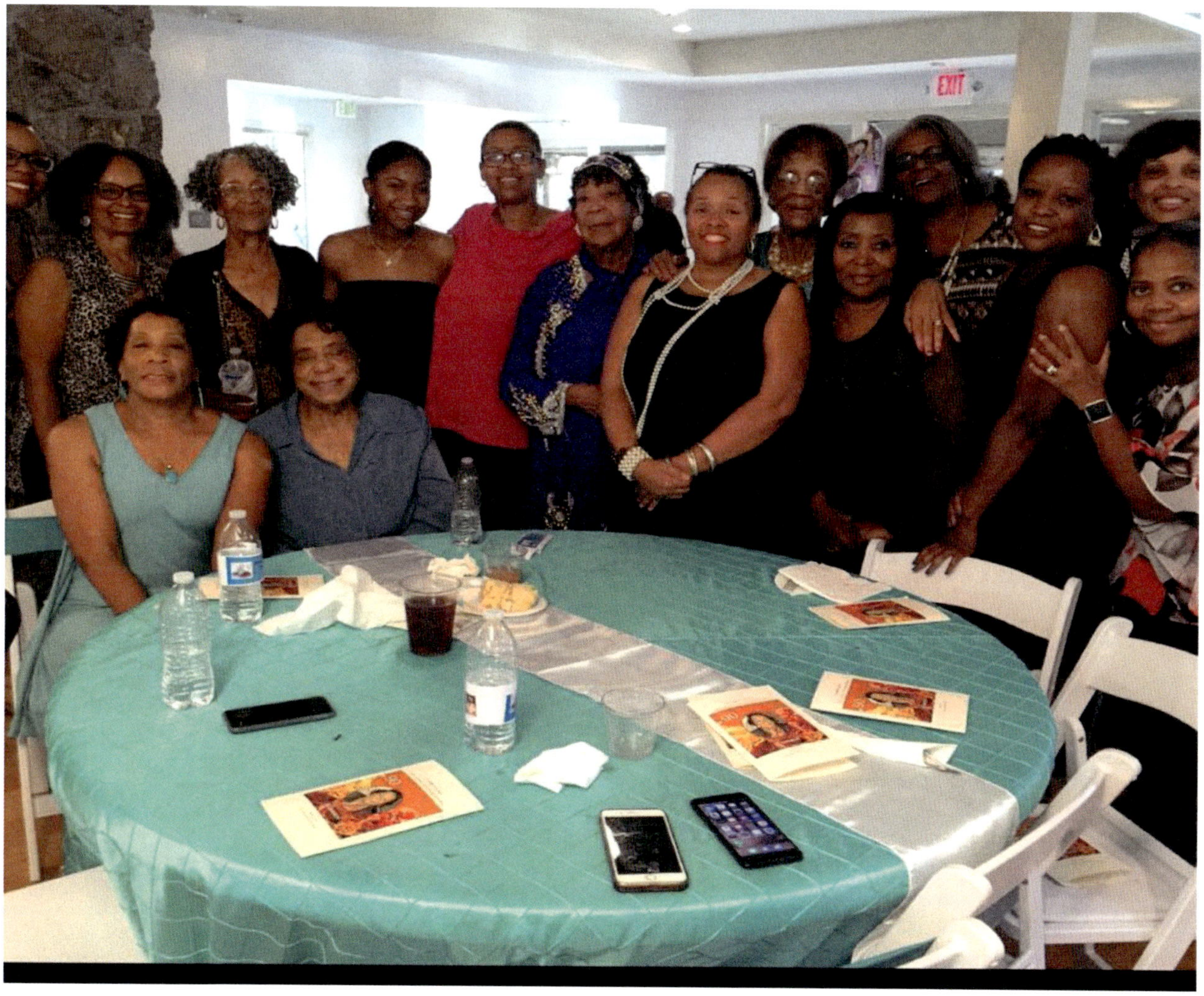
EXIT

CELEBRATION of LIFE, FAITH, LOVE & GRATITUDE

90th Birthday Celebration for Lucille Cameron

October 7, 2017
Maumelle Park on The River

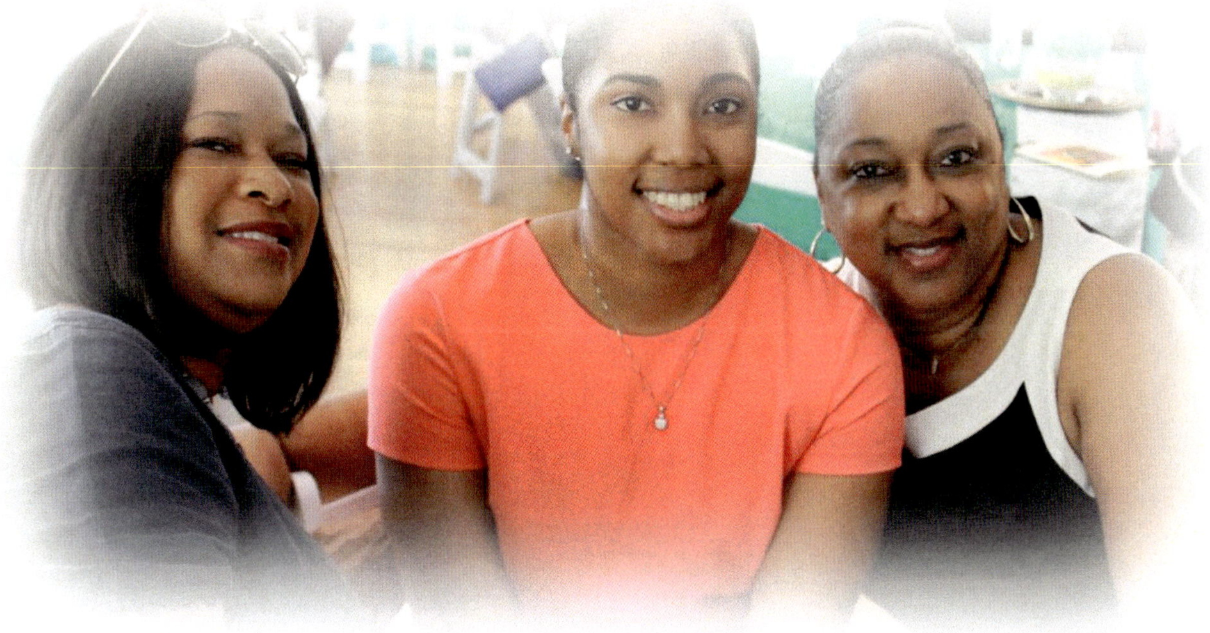

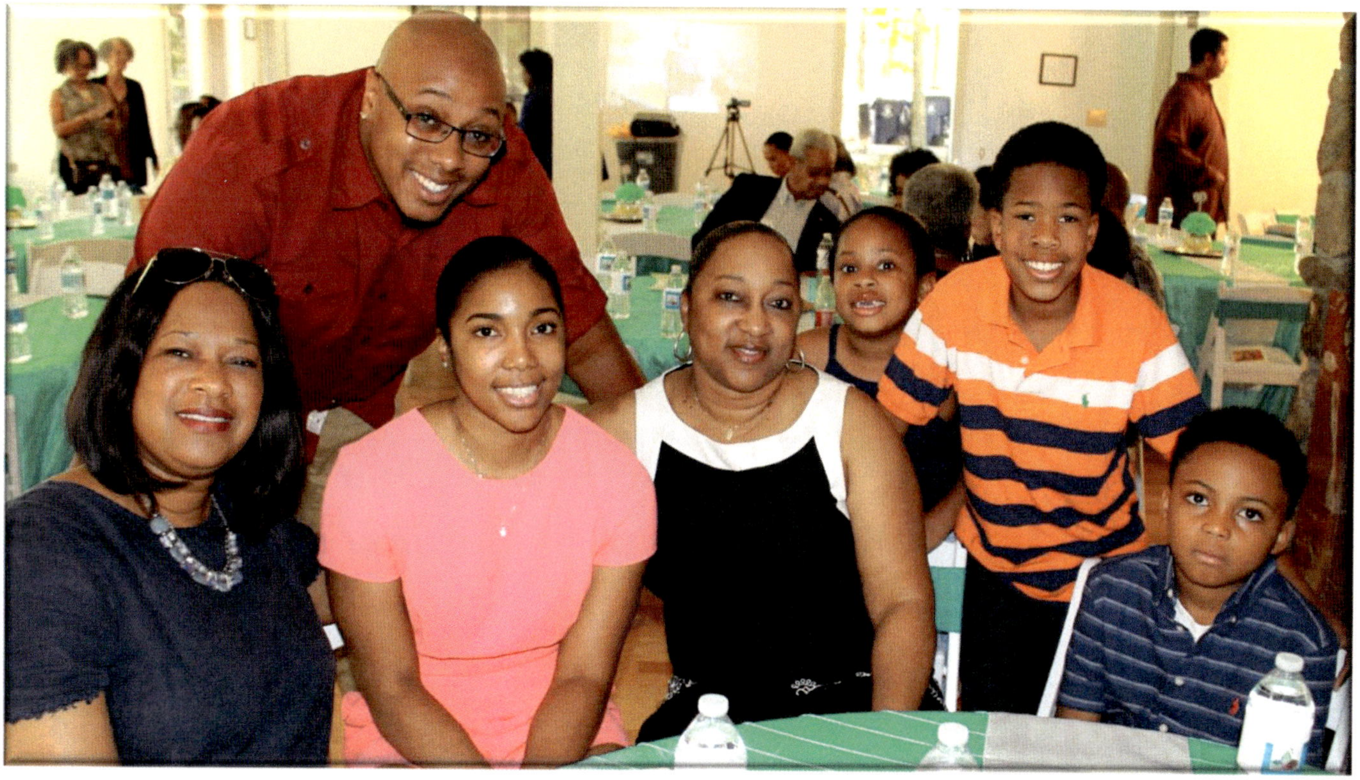

Happy Birthday

Happy Birthday Lucille

90 who?

Lord Look at all these people

Denzel is on his way

He Came

I am proud of you

My Brilliant Grandson

Brothers

We are the younger sisters

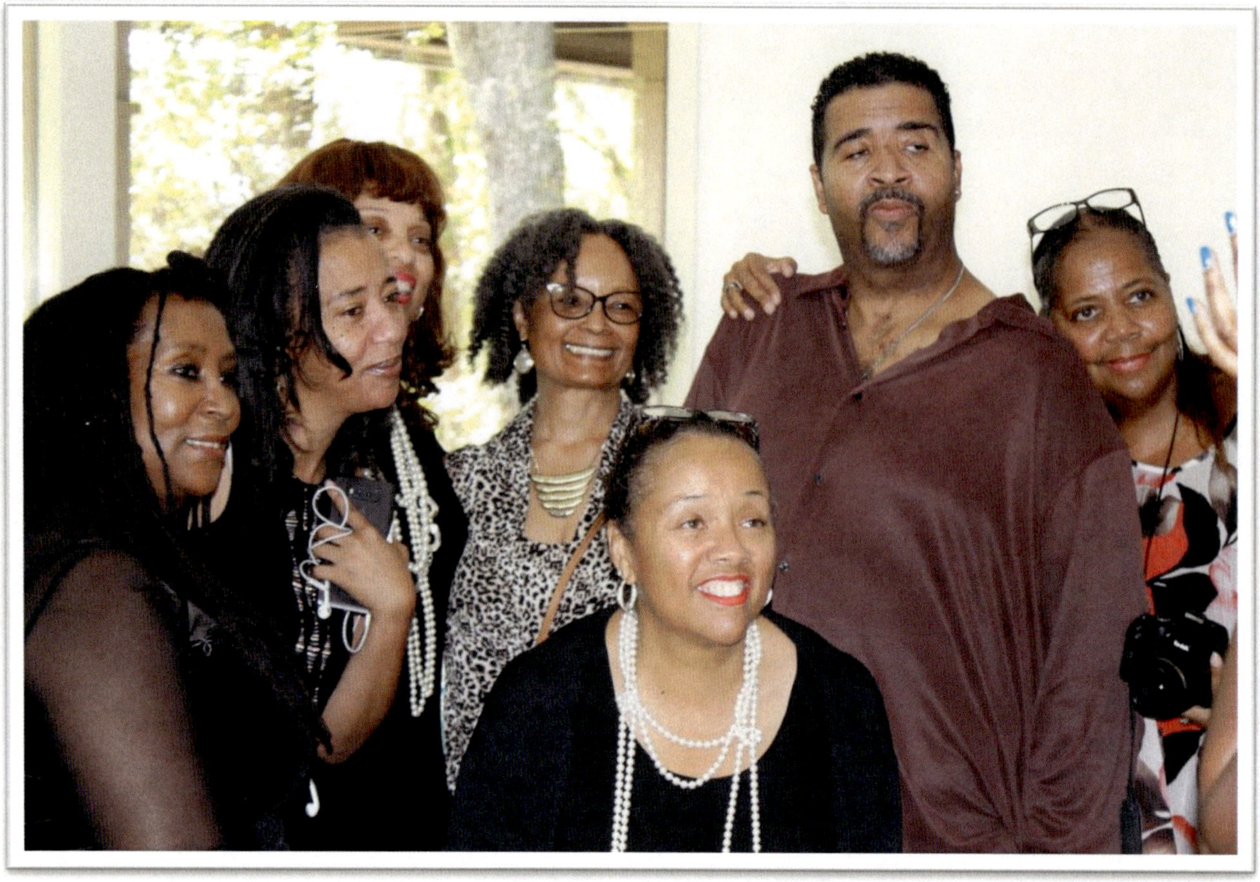

I Hope You Enjoyed My 90th Birthday Party Pics

You are all invited to my 100th

God has allowed me to live for over nine decades, and I thank him daily for his blessings. My children don't want to discuss my funeral plans with them when they call. They try to change the subject. I tell them, how much longer do you think I will live? I have seen a lot in my lifetime, many first and last, too. I have lived through some turbulent times in America and times of peace. 1964, the year the Civil Rights Act was passed, but on April 4, 1968, in Memphis, Tennessee, the personification of the civil rights movement, Dr. Martin Luther King, was assassinated. Change always comes at a price; sometimes, it's the ultimate price. When Barack Obama became president, many considered his presidency a culmination of Martin's dream. The political climate has changed, and we are no longer divided by party affiliation. There is a more significant divide among men. We are separated by the many categories we create, where we place people in sections according to our judgment.

The Apostle Paul decried in Romans 7:24-25 Oh wretched man that I am! Who shall deliver me from the body of this death? 25 I thank God through Jesus Christ our Lord.

There is no political party or appointed leader who will solve the issues and the troubles of today. Sure, we do our civic duty to vote and support our leaders who are true leaders. Paul asked who can deliver us…? The answer can only be found in Jesus Christ. Suppose you have purchased this book or are reading someone else's copy. Let me leave you with the most essential advice written in this book.

Bow your head and ask Jesus to forgive you of your sins. Ask him to come into your heart, help you live this life in a way that is pleasing to him, and, most importantly, give you eternal life with him.

The Bible says in Romans 10:9-10

King James Version

If you confess with your mouth the Lord Jesus and believe that God has raised him from the dead, you will be saved. For with the heart, man believeth unto righteousness, and with the mouth, confession is made unto salvation.

Love You All

Lucille

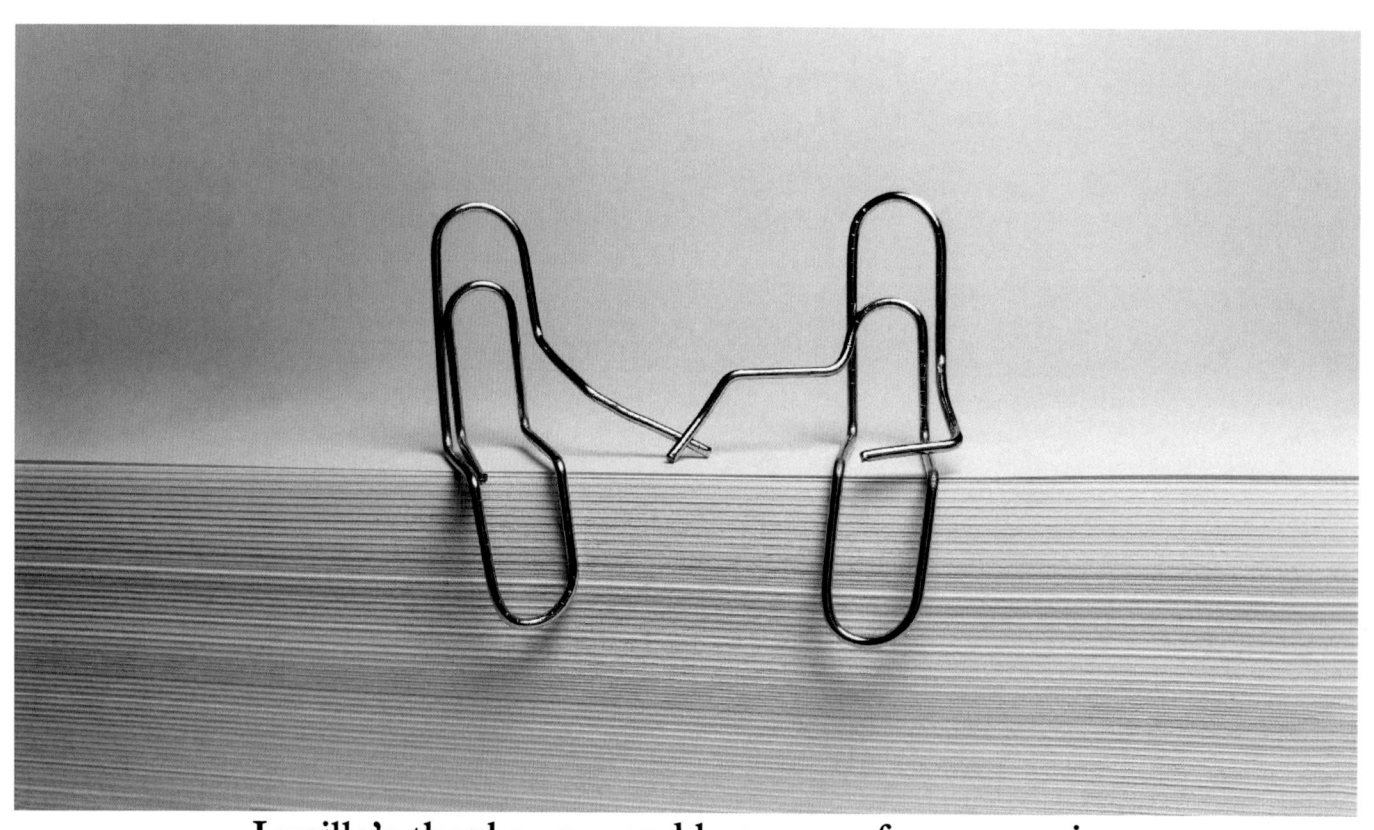

Lucille's thanks you, and here are a few more pics

Lucille's Children, Grandchildren, Great Grandchild and Son-In-Laws

Bobby, although you are not pictured, thank you for all your delicious food!

Lucille & Diane

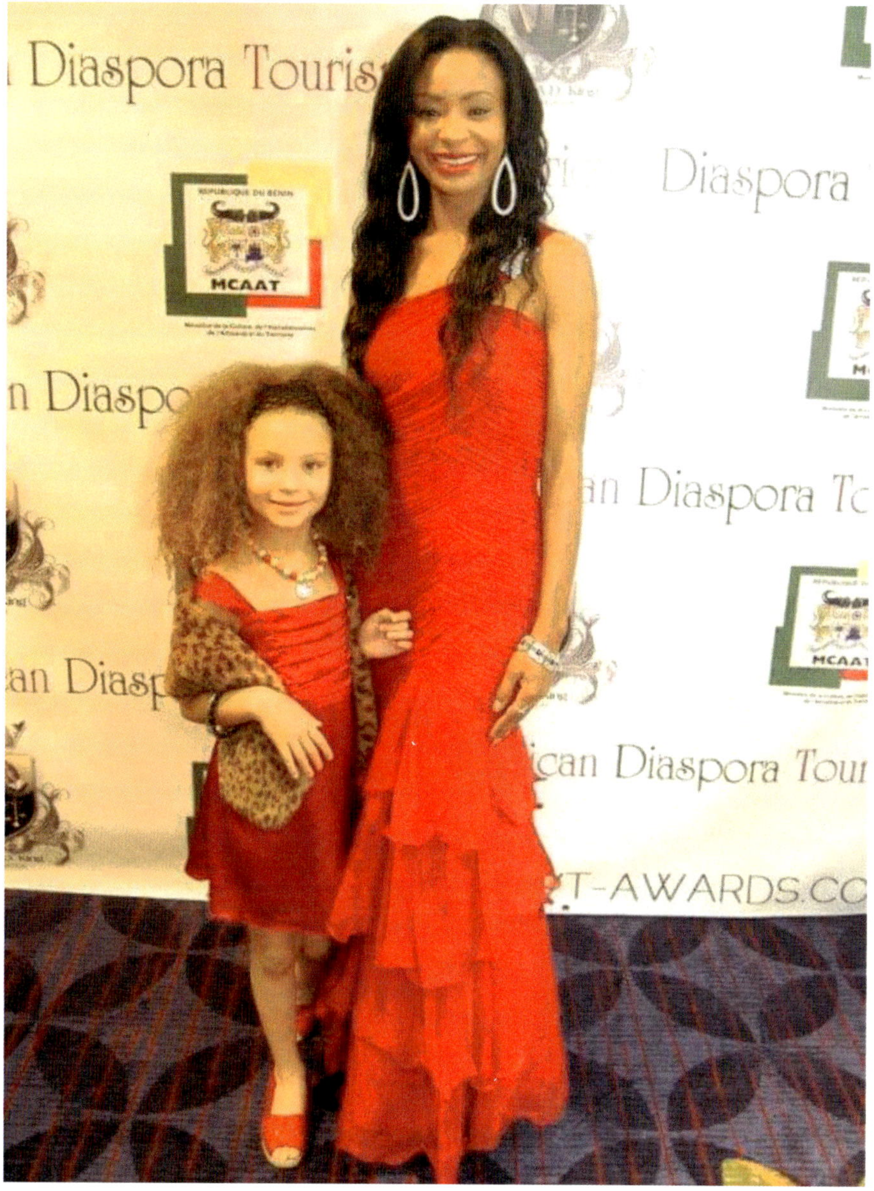
Diaspora
MCAAT

Granddaughters Chardonee and Michaela

Lucille through the years

We love you, Mom, and are proud of your accomplishments.

May this be the first of many books that you write!!!!!

Love

Bonita

Karla

Tonia

Tiffany

Barbara

Diane

Michael

All the Grandchildren

Both the Great Grands

Your Family, Friends, and Special Friends,

Nieces, Nephews, Cousins

Bobby, Robert, Troy, Ed

Brother & Sister In-Laws, Pearl, Bruce, Bertha, Christine, Juana, and

Children's Personal & Social Media Friends

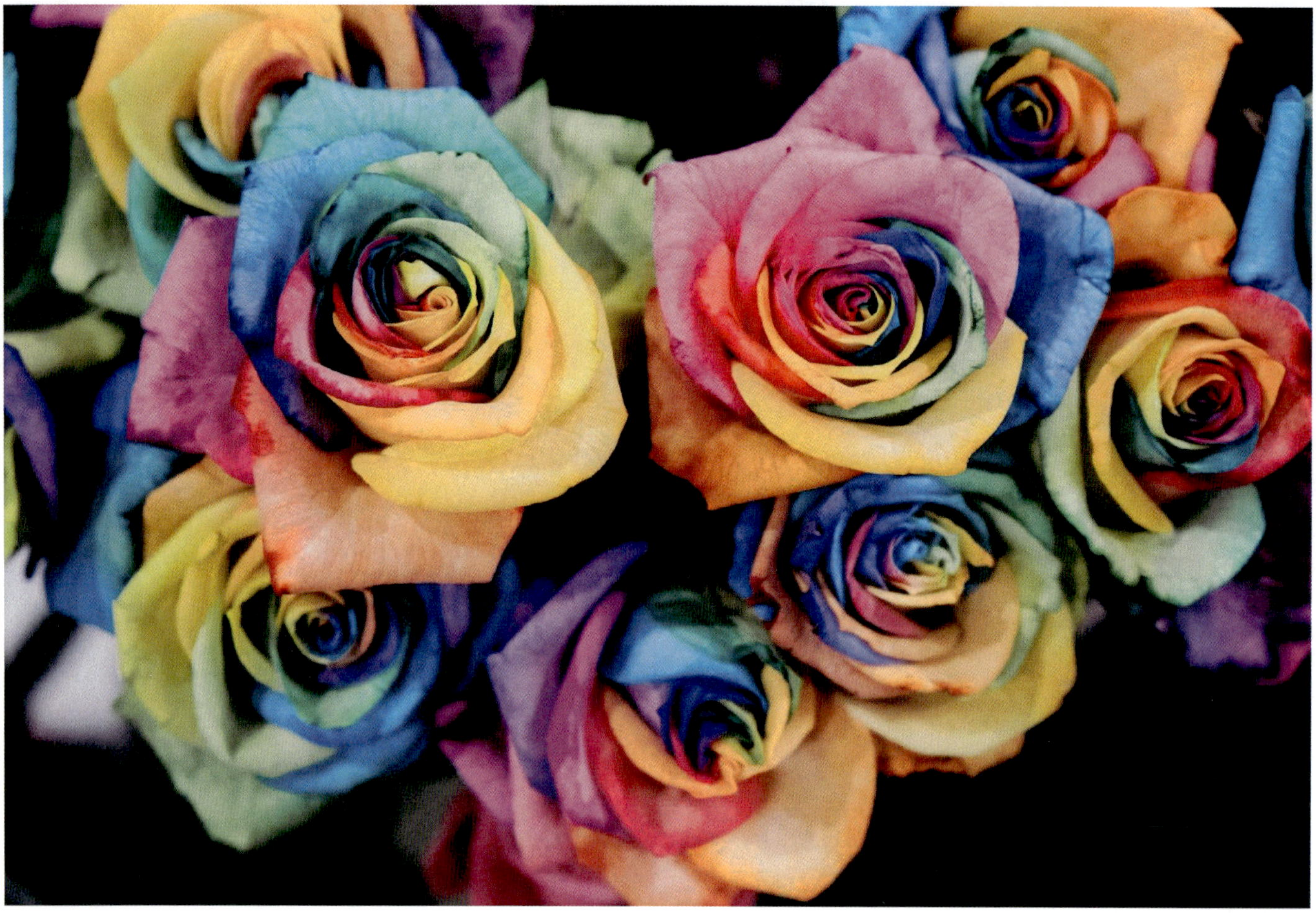

For Bulk Book Orders – thesittingstone@gmail.com

For interviews & Book signings - thesittingstone@gmail.com

Copyright 2024

Some photos stock photos by google
Photo Credits
Donna Morgan Johnson
Bonita Springer
Tonia Powell
Marion Gibson

Made in the USA
Columbia, SC
15 October 2024

bd986b9e-8d67-44b2-8efe-aabf3129ae42R01